BEHAVIOUR BASICS for PARENTS

Giving You the Tools from Schools

TRACEY CAMPBELL

Be the One Press
A division of **Together Transforming Behaviour Ltd**

Copyright © Tracey Campbell 2017

Tracey Campbell has asserted her moral right under the Copyright, Designs and Patents Act 1988 to be identified as the author of this work.

A CIP catalogue record of this book is available from the British Library.

ISBN 978-0-9575302-1-8

This book is a work of non-fiction, however, some of the names, dates, personal details and places have been changed in order to protect the identities of those mentioned in any real-life accounts.

Edited by Jane Collinson
Design & typesetting by Lucy Llewellyn at Head & Heart
Illustrations by Tom Pearce at Drawings of Things
Photography by Leroy Harley

Printed and bound in the UK by 4edge Limited, UK

2 4 6 8 10 9 7 5 3 1

This book is dedicated to **my mum**,
For standing strong and staying hopeful.

Contents

Acknowledgements

First of all, I express my thanks to the families who took part in Channel 4's *Mr Drew's School for Boys*. Your courage and commitment to the Behaviour Basics Programme was exceptional. Thank you for trusting me enough to let me into your worlds.

Thank you Channel 4 and Ricochet for the opportunity to be a part of the show. It was by far one of the highlights of my professional career to date.

Mum, thank you for never giving up on me when the going got tough and you had far more questions than answers. Thank you for believing that I would come good in the end.

Grace Owen, you are second to none. You have been an amazing coach and I am truly grateful to have had you by my side throughout the writing of this second book. Your patience, creative input and proofreading have helped me tremendously.

Jackie Pathay, thank you for your help with proofreading and for being a constant source of encouragement and enthusiasm as the book neared completion.

Christine Kinnear, thank you for your precision and care with proofreading.

Tiffany Adonis-French, thank you for being such a sterling example of a mum. What a remarkable job you have done with your boys. I've been watching and taking notes! You are an inspiration!

....

....

To head teachers Peter Lewis and Martha Braithwaite thank you for believing so passionately in my Behaviour Basics Programme; working with the parents at your schools was an honour.

Thank you to Jane Collinson for an outstanding job with the copy editing and to Tom Pearce for bringing your amazing artwork to another one of my titles.

Thanks to Lucy Llewellyn for the text and cover design; it was great working with you.

To the readers of *Behaviour Basics for Parents*, may this book provide just what you need to parent with increased confidence and insight into your children's behaviour.

....

Introduction

We work with children, you live with children

Let's work together

Dane was seven years old and belonged to a group of very lively boys in my Year Two class. They were inseparable and I loved watching their camaraderie as it played out in the classroom from day to day. Dane was not a difficult child at all, so I was somewhat taken aback by the account I received from his mum, Carol one day about his behaviour at home.

'I'm just finding it really difficult,' she began. 'Dane's behaviour at home is getting worse. He's becoming more and more defiant and only seems to listen when I shout.'

The problems ranged from Dane spending prolonged periods of time on his game console to refusing to go to bed when asked. It was clear from Carol's report that he had no regard for her authority.

'Even when I threaten to take his console away, he just laughs. I find it so rude. If I'm honest, Miss Campbell, I don't really know what to do. That's why I wanted to speak to you to find out how you deal with this kind of behaviour at school.'

What I found interesting, as I listened, was that there were a lot of threats about sanctions, but none of these were actually carried out. When I enquired about the rules and routines within the home Carol said there were none. She appeared surprised at my enquiry, as if these things had never crossed her mind.

I gave her a brief outline of our approaches to behaviour or more specifically misbehaviour at school.

I explained that, for us, it begins with a clear set of rules displayed in every classroom and known by all children and adults. For example:

- Follow instructions
- Stay on task
- Respect people and property

- Keep hands and feet to yourselves
- Be in the right place at the right time

When children know what is expected, it is easier to hold them to account.

Closely linked to the rules is an agreed system of rewards and sanctions. Rewards consist of stickers, certificates, extra playtime, extended time on the computer and free-choice activity sessions at the end of the week. Sanctions could be any of the following: time out in class, time out in another class, loss of playtime or lunchtime detention. So, not only do children know in advance what behaviour is expected, they also know what happens when these expectations are not met. In fact, we say to children 'If you choose the behaviour, you choose the consequence that goes with it.'

What became clear from our conversation was that though Carol had made some attempt to establish routines, the concept of rules was foreign. Not only were there no clear guidelines about what constituted acceptable behaviour, the sanctions were things she simply made up on the spot – they were reactive and often over the top. Carol had not given prior thought to consequences and was therefore operating in panic mode. This led to a mis-match between the behaviour and the consequence. She told me of the time Dane was banned from playing his game console for one month because he did not hang up his school uniform as asked. Upon further reflection, Carol realised that a month ban was excessive particularly because Dane was not playing with the console when he should have been dealing with his uniform – he had simply forgotten to hang it up.

'I wasn't thinking about the appropriateness of the

consequence,' she admitted. 'I was angry and I just wanted Dane to see that I am in charge.'

I advised Carol to have a conversation with Dane about the behaviour she had begun to notice at home. Children often notice the shift: the change in the atmosphere and the tension that begins to mount in the home. They notice when parents are angrier than usual – particularly if this includes shouting. I suggested this conversation should culminate in agreement about what was acceptable at home and in the establishment of some agreed rules, such as:

- Follow instructions the first time
- Hand in game console at bedtime
- Speak the way you want to be spoken to
- Complete tasks without being asked

This conversation was the first of many as I began to coach Carol through the establishment and then enforcement of rules. We met over a course of weeks and though progress was slow, things were moving in the right direction. It took both Carol and Dane a while to become accustomed to the new rules within the home; but once mum became more consistent, progress was accelerated. Dane became more independent – adhering to agreed routines without being reminded. In addition, Carol reported that Dane was slowly beginning to accept her instructions without answering back, which was a huge step forward.

What had certainly made a difference for Dane was the knowledge that there was constant dialogue between his mum and adults at school. This was important for Dane because not only were consistent approaches now being used in school and at home, but he was also receiving recognition from both places for his efforts to amend his behaviour. I also took the opportunity during this process to challenge Dane about the fact that there was such a huge difference between his behaviour at school and how he behaved at home. I simply reminded Dane at home time of the success he had experienced at school and the expectation that his positive attitude would continue at home.

I set the expectation that I wanted to hear he was making good choices at home just like he did at school. I also stressed the importance of showing the same respect to his mum that he showed to me and other adults in school.

The collaboration between school and home worked wonders for Dane. It was as if he began to feel he was letting himself down by not complying at home as he did at school. He loved the praise he received at school for his good work and behaviour; he became more and more keen to give his mum plenty of reasons to praise him at home. The fact that Dane's change in behaviour was met with praise and recognition from mum was very significant because it broke the cycle that had been established. Dane was now receiving positive attention for doing the right thing rather than negative attention for doing the wrong thing.

'The rules provided something for us to refer back to,' Carol said. 'I found I was nagging him less and simply pointing him towards the agreed rules, which were displayed on the fridge and in his room.'

It was conversations like these that really got me thinking about the links between school and home and particularly how I, as a teacher, could make that link stronger and more meaningful. Much of what teachers do in school around behaviour management would prove hugely beneficial to any parent because our practices are focused much more on preventing poor behaviour than fixing it. Our systems and approaches are designed to create environments that are conducive to positive behaviour: expectations are clear and when these are met there is acknowledgement.

Behaviour Basics for Parents is about prevention and collaboration. It seeks to give parents the tools from schools so there is greater cohesion and exchange between the two environments where children spend most of their time – home and school. School is a child's first introduction to the world; if they cannot function there, how will they function in wider society? The need for strong partnerships between school and home is pressing because parents can either help or hinder the work that teachers carry out to prepare children for their place in the world. Children are the messengers of what is happening at home; their behaviour tells us if things are going well or if something needs work.

My intention is to share my experiences as a teacher, consultant and also what I gleaned from being the resident behaviour consultant on Channel 4's *Mr Drew's School for Boys*; a four-week summer school designed to help parents regain control of their sons. I would also like to open the school gates and offer parents an insight into how we, as teachers, manage the issues that emerge there with children's behaviour. By explaining our approaches within school, I can provide strategies and solutions as you, as a parent or carer, face these very same issues at home.

The book sets out the concerns as they emerge in schools and then details how teachers respond to them. It then places the issue within the home context and provides some ideas as to how parents can respond.

I want to highlight just how important addressing

behaviour is; and help parents to avoid waiting until things go wrong before they talk about it. The book will provide insight into what behaviour is and why misbehaviour occurs. The reality is that we all (adults and children alike) display behaviours, which are a form of communication. Part of my objective is to help parents accept that they have to *be* what they wish to *see* in their children. Parenting must be a mixture of modelling and instructing.

I will explore some of the problems parents face around discipline and look at where love fits into this. I will also address the importance of consistency within the home: not just continuing to apply what has been agreed but, even more important, both parents consistently transmitting the same message.

I have seen first-hand the effect on children when they do not get off to a good start in the morning; it quickly shows up in their attitude and behaviour. I will share some poignant stories of children with whom I have worked; they arrive at school worried or harassed simply because of the pace of the morning dash.

My experience working with parents on *Mr Drew's School for Boys* was incredibly enjoyable and really opened my eyes to the need for strong partnerships, caring approaches and an open-door policy. With their permission I will share many of their stories – including the anguish and the guilt they carried as the parent of the 'naughty' child. The sense of hopelessness that many of them experienced was palpable. Being able to deepen their understanding and provide solutions was an incredibly satisfying experience for me.

It is my hope that through this book I can do the same for you: broaden your understanding of behaviour, how it develops and how it is displayed by children. As adults we need to respond so children receive a clear message about agreed expectations while ensuring that communication of these is not lost through heightened emotions.

The book ends with an interesting perspective: that of my mother. Like the parents at Mr Drew's summer school, she found herself parenting a problematic child – me! I hope this chapter will serve as a beacon of hope and will take the reader on a journey from despair to delight. My mum's story will resonate with many and will hopefully show that troublesome children can press through their difficulties and find their place within the world.

You live with children, I work with children. I am convinced that through the pages of *Behaviour Basics for Parents* we can create stronger connections between these two worlds that will lead to improved behaviour, happier homes, increased attainment at school – and to successful living for children throughout their schools years and beyond.

Chapter One

Behaviour speaks, are you listening?

A look at what children's behaviour tells us

Behaviour is an action or reaction to an internal feeling or the words and actions of others

Understanding that behaviour is a form of communication is a key starting point for parents. In fact, it is how we all alert the world to what we want and need. Behaviour is not exclusive to children. As adults we have all established behaviour patterns and have learnt over time how to use these behaviours to get our emotional needs met, control the outcome of an event or hide what we are really feeling.

So, if a child feels angry they may throw something or stamp their feet in response. Or if a child's request for another biscuit has been declined they may begin to cry, not because they are in genuine pain but simply because they do not like what they have been told. The child who cries when they have been told no may have learnt that when they cry mummy or daddy will give in and let them have their way.

A friend of mine recently told me that when her three-year-old daughter was asked by her granny why she was crying, she replied, 'Because mummy and daddy will not let me have my way!'

This can be a major challenge for parents and carers: the idea of being uncomfortable when their child cries. It can arouse feelings of guilt when an action or inaction on the part of a parent has reduced a child to tears. Some tears are, indeed, about genuine distress, hurt, pain and upset. It is imperative, however, that parents know the difference between tears of pain and tears of protest! There will be more about this in the next chapter, 'How do you spell love'?

Behaviour is a form of communication. It is therefore important that we both listen to and understand what is being 'said' through behaviour to ensure that our responses are targeting the root issue and yielding the kind of outcome we seek. The response of parents is key to the whole process of managing and shaping behaviour because a situation can very easily be escalated or de-escalated depending on the response of an adult.

Behaviour can, of course, be both positive and negative, helpful and unhelpful. Children will express feelings relating to joy and jealousy, excitement and embarrassment as well as letting us know if they feel bored or ignored. It is misbehaviour, however, that leaves many parents feeling bewildered and embarrassed. With the best will in the world a number of parents find themselves at a complete loss as to what to do.

Why does misbehaviour occur?

Children misbehave for a number of reasons many of which are linked to their attempts to **attain** or **avoid** something.

Children generally misbehave to:

- Seek attention
- Gain a sense of control
- Test boundaries/express disagreement
- Control the outcome of a situation

Let us look at each of these roots of misbehaviour in more detail.

Seeking attention

Attention seeking is usually the primary driver for misbehaviour. Children are skilled at using their behaviour to demand and monopolise the attention of their parents.

The need for attention is perfectly legitimate as we all need the affirmation that comes from being noticed and praised; but parents must be wise and avoid falling for the unconscious schemes children use to achieve their goal for attention.

Children love to be noticed and attended to by their parents. Young children, in particular, are by nature self-centred, which is very much in keeping with their age and stage of development. Therefore, when they are engrossed in a play activity on their own, they will quite happily entertain themselves for a time but, after a while, they begin to crave engagement and need the contact and attention of a key adult, whether they are close by or far away.

This example of attention seeking is healthy and is not the kind of scenario that parents outline to me when talking about their children's behaviour. What parents report are accounts of children pretending to cry when requests are made of them; in some cases this progresses to shouting and screaming. Whining and sulking is another form of attention-seeking behaviour that parents often talk about; the objective here is often to change the parent's no to a yes!

Misbehaviour is usually rare when children live in an environment where there are clear expectations and where they receive validation when these are met. The problem in many homes, however, is that parents and carers often do not talk about behaviour with their children until things start to go wrong. Parents only then notice the behaviour because it is now extreme. While the child was behaving in accordance with expectations and instructions they provided little or no recognition or affirmation to the child. This is the big mistake that many parents make; they only talk about behaviour when they have been forced to. Rather than making expectations for positive behaviour explicit and praising children when these are met, they often leave children to work things out for themselves with little guidance.

It is vital that parents help children understand the impact of their behaviour: *why* it's not helpful, and *why* mummy or daddy are not happy. Conversely, when children play cooperatively, speak politely or do their chores without being reminded – praise lets them know that their parents are pleased. This serves as encouragement for the child to do more of the same.

Some children appear to have an insatiable appetite for attention and need constant contact with adults. It is usually these children who learn that negative behaviour brings adult attention.

The extreme end of attention-seeking behaviour occurs when a child has learnt that when they display certain types of poor behaviour it is very difficult for an adult to ignore it. They use such behaviour to, in many ways, force the hand of the adults in their lives to attend to them. Children caught in this cycle are usually those for whom experiencing quality time with an adult is a rarity. They do not readily receive the attention that they need, so they use negative behaviour to achieve it.

In her book, *The Incredible Years*, Carolyn Webster-Stratton says:

> ... children will work for attention from others, especially parents, whether it is positive (praise) or negative (criticism) in nature. If they do not receive positive attention, then they will strive for negative attention since that is better than none at all.
>
> (Carolyn Webster-Stratton,
> *The Incredible Years*, 2005, p.18)

It is vital that parents understand just how important positive attention is for children. The extent to which children are prepared to go to achieve any form of attention makes the point very clear.

Attention seeking and me

I recall being a very attention-seeking child, much more at school than at home. I learnt very early on that my attempts at gaining adult attention at school were far more successful than they were at home. So that was where I focused my energies. I can clearly remember throwing myself on the floor at nursery; then, once an adult came to attend to me I would intensify my tantrum because I did not want the adult attention to stop. I have similar memories of school: needing to be first, always wanting to get things right and constantly needing the reassurance that my teachers had me in their gaze.

I must have been around seven years old and my mum had purchased some new trainers for me. I was so chuffed with my new footwear that I would not take them off. A cousin came to visit later that day and I remember following her all around the house. I was desperate for her to notice my new shoes, but my attempts kept on failing. As I sat alongside her on the window sill I decided that I would keep swinging my legs higher and higher until she noticed my shoes. Finally she belted out, 'Oh, that's why you keep following me around; you've got new shoes!' Mission accomplished: that was all I needed to hear. I just needed someone to notice.

I got involved in many negative behaviour incidences during both my primary and secondary schooling. I learnt that my disruptive behaviour brought recognition, that my rudeness to adults brought indignation and that I could command an audience with one simple prank or misdemeanour. I therefore spent my days defying adults and entertaining peers.

Gaining a sense of control

Sometimes children's misbehaviour is about a need for power and control. They will try to control the outcome of a situation or display partial compliance to exert a degree of control. Have you ever asked your son or daughter to do something in the home and though they do not refuse outright, they comply on their own terms and in their own time? You call them and though they come, they come very slowly. You ask them to pick up the toys and though they get down onto the floor, they tie their shoelaces before they start to pick anything up. They do this to exercise some control over how and when the task is carried out.

This kind of behaviour is closely linked with testing boundaries, which is actually a very natural part of being a child. I know that many parents probably do not want to hear that, but I'm afraid it is perfectly natural for children to test boundaries – sorry! The much bigger issue is what happens when the boundary is pushed, but we will explore more about that when we discuss limit setting in chapter seven.

The kind of power-seeking behaviour I see usually falls into one of two categories: where a child has no sense of control; or where they have been allowed control and do not want to relinquish it.

Looking for power

This kind of power-seeking behaviour stems from a child feeling as though their lives are out of control. They feel the world is an unpredictable and at times scary place. These children need to gain a sense of control from somewhere so they seek to use their behaviour to achieve it. They have a need to feel significant and in charge, often because they somehow feel inferior or unimportant. This can be because of family pressures arising from financial or relational difficulties. The arrival of a new sibling can make children feel unsettled and question their position within the family.

As well as the attention-seeking difficulties mentioned above, as a child I also struggled with power-seeking behaviour, which stemmed from a need to feel significant. The more siblings that were born into my family, the less emotional availability there was for me. These feelings affected my behaviour at school in a major way.

I once incurred an after-school detention because I had not submitted my maths homework. I was one of a number of girls who rocked up to the maths classroom after school feeling aggrieved and intent on causing trouble. Upon arrival I could see that my maths teacher, Miss Godwin was talking to a visitor, who I later discovered was from a local bank. We were instructed to wait in the corridor until she had finished her conversation; but I had other intentions. I was not going to wait quietly. I was going to create a commotion and force my teacher to end her conversation prematurely. Respect was not high on my agenda, and this was a prime opportunity for me to exert power and control. I was going to take it.

'She's taking liberties!' I bellowed, loud enough for her to hear me from inside the classroom.

'What does she mean "wait outside"? I was here on time and she needs to start this detention on time.' By now the other girls were becoming riled up – my attempts to dominate and disrupt were working. I continued my rant, forcing Miss Godwin to come out and address me.

'How dare you be so rude in front of a visitor,' she scolded. She tried hard to keep her voice low but her red face spoke volumes. I levelled the same allegation at her.

'How dare you be so rude and have us waiting out here. You are wasting our time!' My school friends were visibly shocked at my rudeness, but I was feeling bigger and bigger by the second.

We went back and forth. I felt I had to finish what I had started or run the risk of looking silly in front of my friends.

Miss Godwin was left with no choice but to re-enter the classroom and terminate the meeting with her visitor from the bank. Predictably, that detention was only the beginning of my troubles once my behaviour was reported to the headmistress.

The feeling of control I gained from these displays of defiance was so fulfilling that, despite the harsh consequences, I regularly found myself in trouble for refusing to follow an adult's instructions.

Holding onto power

The second form of power-seeking behaviour is displayed by children who do not want to relinquish control because they have always been allowed to control situations. Let me use a real story to make the point.

If you have seen *Mr Drew's School for Boys*, you may recall Zane and his parents, Alan and Michelle. By his mother's own admission, Zane ruled the roost. He dictated his bath time, bedtime, wake-up time; you name it, he was in charge. When children have this much control over their lives it can be very difficult for them to yield to the authority of any adult, because in their world they do as they please. So they continue to seek power in situations because those are the rules of engagement they have been accustomed to: I am in charge, I do what I like and I do not have to listen to you.

In the case of Michelle and Alan, they had to slowly take back the control they had given over to their son. Part of my job was to help them understand that Zane was not going to give up his 'throne' without a fight.

'We are trying to implement the strategies, particularly around bedtime routines, but it just turns into a shouting match,' Michelle reported.

I asked her what she thought all the shouting and screaming on Zane's part was about. Michelle paused for a moment and said, 'We have changed and he doesn't like it. He's fighting us because he wants to continue to have his way.' Michelle realised that what she had now become embroiled in was a power play – Zane fighting to hold on to what he has always had, while Michelle and Alan were fighting to recapture what they had lost.

This was a huge realisation for Alan and Michelle. It helped them to understand that they were engaged in a battle they had to win.

The spoilt child

So you see, some control-seeking behaviour comes from children's experiences of uncertainty, of change and powerlessness within their home and relationships. Other control-seeking behaviour has been brought about because of passive parenting: where parents and children have swapped roles. Often, when people see a bossy or spoilt child they comment that it is cute. But, if we really consider what it means for a child to be spoilt we will see that it is neither cute nor clever; particularly in the longer term when they become teenagers or adults, by which time the behaviour is really unpleasant.

The word 'spoilt' actually means 'to impair, damage, or harm, the character or nature of (someone) by unwise treatment or excessive indulgence'. (www.dictionary.com)

I have never met a parent who deliberately wanted to do any of the above to their child. However, through allowing a child to have power and control beyond their years, they are in fact spoiling that child, which is damaging. It can harm the child's development because they grow accustomed to a set of rules that are only applicable within their home. They therefore struggle with authority figures in school where the control they are accustomed to at home is not given.

Please be clear: spoiling children is not a laughing matter. Just imagine a spoilt adult at work, in a team or in the community. It is not a pretty picture.

Testing boundaries

As stated earlier, it is perfectly natural for a child to test boundaries: to see if your no really is no. Children will neglect to do what you have asked to see if you will insist or relent. It can be very empowering for a child to win in a situation of boundary testing. The more episodes of success they have the more they will want to repeat it. To get one over on an authority figure is a significant achievement for a child.

Be very clear about where you place the boundary lines within your home because you will have to exert a lot of energy into ensuring that they are held firmly in place. For this reason, it is not wise to mimic what others do in their home purely because it appears to be common practice or works for them. Do not put yourself in a position where you are fighting to uphold something that you do not really believe in. Parenting is hard enough!

When discussing boundary testing with a friend of mine, she said, 'What my son does is sing when he is brushing his teeth, and I know he is simply trying to prolong things. Another tool in his armoury is to eat extra slowly when he is told to hurry up!'

Children will test boundaries in a whole host of ways. Here are some examples:

- Eating in their rooms when they know the rule is no food in bedrooms
- Staying out a little later than agreed
- Playing on a game console longer than was agreed
- Having a snack before dinner when they know the rule is no snacks before dinner
- Not taking off their school uniform when that has always been the routine
- Saying no!
- Taking a few more steps before following an instruction to come

Yes, children will sometimes go as far as saying no to an instruction to see what you are going to do. In these situations, the parent's response is so important. A child needs to be left in no doubt that when you give an instruction you expect it to be carried out. If the child persists and will not comply after a number of attempts, the matter should be left for the time being, but it must be revisited later and a consequence imposed for non-compliance. While it may be natural for children to test boundaries, it is necessary for parents to ensure that the boundaries do not move. A child needs to get a clear message from an adult: you can kick, you can scream, you can roll around, but my no is still no.

BEHAVIOUR BASICS FOR PARENTS

Controlling the outcome of a situation

Misbehaviour is often about trying to avoid or to attain something. Children have a number of strategies that they have learnt in order to avoid having to do as they have been told. It becomes problematic, as was the case with Zane, when children have experienced success using such strategies and know that if they shout loud enough, for long enough, mum and dad will back down.

I am convinced that the primary objective of most temper tantrums is to control the outcome of a situation. Think about the last time your child had a temper tantrum. I strongly suspect that it began with you saying something that your son or daughter did not want to hear. Am I right? Then a tantrum ensued and the aim was simple: to change your no to a yes – now! Children have a way of making something appear very urgent and catastrophic as though, if you don't buy that sweet in the supermarket, the sky is going to fall in or they will die of starvation! The desire to have the sweet is visceral and the fury that you will not grant that request is even stronger.

In her book, *The Incredible Years*, Carolyn Webster-Stratton uses a powerful analogy about control that she calls The Vending Machine. She explains what it can be like for a child who has had some degree of success with being able to control outcomes by wearing parents down. When parents decide to address the issue by taking back control and holding the boundaries, it can be as if the child has made their regular trip to the vending machine but something different happens...

The child goes to the machine to make their usual purchase of Champs Chocolate. However, on this occasion they put the pound coin in and nothing happens. The child proceeds to press the refund button, but the machine does not release the coin. The child then tries to shake the machine but still no chocolate. He then gives the machine a kick: still no chocolate. Liken this to a child making a request of a parent and the child being told no. Carolyn explains that this is what happens when a child approaches a parent who is trying to hold the boundaries. The parent says no, but the child still insists. Not wanting to give in the child tries shouting, then swearing, then crying – and still no joy.

Finally, the child turns away from the machine having accepted that it is not going to release the chocolate. Just as they begin to walk away, however, they hear 'kuplunk!' The sound of a Champs Chocolate falling into the collection tray.

This is the same aim for children who use their behaviour to control the outcome of events. They will try every which way to get you to 'release' what it is that they want. Even though you have said no, they have learnt that if they keep on, they will eventually hear 'kuplunk': the sound of resignation, the sound of deflation – the sound of victory.

Things to think about and do...

♦ When does misbehaviour generally occur in your house? Is there a pattern? Think about:

◊ Time of day
◊ Who is usually involved?
◊ What is the trigger?

♦ Have you considered what is acceptable behaviour in your home? How are these expectations communicated?

♦ Are you consistent at saying yes/no/wait; and sticking to it?

♦ Which of the behaviours mentioned do you observe in your child or children?

Chapter Two

How do you spell love?

*The importance of combining
discipline with love*

The word 'discipline' actually means to teach, not punish

Many parents struggle with the idea and even more so with the application of discipline. For some, their views have been shaped by their own childhood experiences at the hands of authoritative parents, who ruled with a rod of iron. For others, they are simply uncomfortable placing restrictions around their children for fear that it will in some way hinder their development. Nothing could be further from the truth.

Discipline is simply about training and steering a child in the right direction: providing clear guidance about rights and wrongs, dos and don'ts. Without it, children are left to raise themselves, the results of which are catastrophic for the child, parent, school and wider society. A child who has lived without boundaries will struggle to work within agreed parameters at school and later in the workplace.

This feeling of discomfort around enforcing discipline comes, I believe, from the misconception that discipline and love are somehow incompatible. When in reality, discipline does not work without love and love is deficient without discipline. Many of us have memories of an approach to discipline that often left us feeling unloved – as if our parents in that moment had very strong feelings of dislike for us because of what we had said or done. This is not an ideal approach to discipline. Children learn best when discipline is administered in a calm, loving manner. This enables the child to engage fully with what is being said rather than getting lost in the emotion, and sometimes rage, on the part of parents.

We must accept that discipline is appropriate, in fact, that it is vital. There is no other way to raise healthy, balanced children who have a clear sense of what constitutes acceptable behaviour at home and school.

I recall a piece of work I did with a parent called Eilene. She struggled to discipline her sons because she was trying too hard not to be the disciplinarian that her own mother had been.

Eilene's story

'My mum was quite strict with us when we were growing up and I suppose I didn't want to repeat that with my children,' Eilene told me. 'I have memories of being scared to put a foot wrong, so when it came to my own children I went to the other extreme. We don't really have rules in our house and I know now that my boys use whining and shouting to get what they want. Once they start to cry and whine about things I just give in; they know that I can only take so much of the noise. Now that I think about it, I have actually taught them that. I have taught them that if they shout and whine long enough I will eventually let them have their way. At times I even say, "Oh, go on then. I can't take any more of your whining."'

Like many parents, Eilene struggled to say no to her two boys. As they got older the sound of their protests became highly annoying and frustrating for Eilene; but as young boys she had found the sound of them crying most upsetting. She associated the crying with pain and distress and would avoid these encounters as much as possible. That avoidance manifested itself in always saying yes and being overly apologetic if the boys became distressed because of something she had said or had attempted to withhold from them.

Eilene's story is not unique. So now, a question for you: How do *you* spell love? What I mean by this, is what have you told yourself you must do or not do to ensure that your children feel loved by you? Do you spell love Y-E-S? Have you decided that no is a word your children will not hear from you? Do you spell love N-O-W, believing that delay will in some ways cause damage? Do you respond to your child immediately fearing that if they have to wait and become distressed it will not be good for them? How about the spelling D-O N-O-T C-R-Y? This is a very big issue for a lot of parents; the sound of their child crying is something that they just cannot bear.

Misspellings

Let us take a closer look at each of these 'misspellings'.

Y-E-S

The problem with all of these 'misspellings' is that they give children a false impression of the world in which they live. At home mummy and daddy may often say yes, but at play group, in school and when around other family members and friends they will meet people who will have no trouble saying no – and what happens then? A child cannot be blamed for expecting all adults to be like their parents; they are too young to make the distinction. Whatever the established code of conduct is at home, children will expect the same from other adults; they will become distressed and confused when other adults do not play according to the same rules.

Of equal importance, is the fact that children do not learn how to manage the feelings aroused by disappointment when they are pandered to at home. When their every request is met with a yes they are ill-equipped to deal with times when their request is denied; this becomes earth-shattering for the child. Children should be able to bounce back from being told no. Development of a child's resilience is stunted when their requests are always met with a yes.

I have met many parents in my work who, though they understand the importance of saying no, struggle because saying no somehow has negative connotations. They believe that their child will think that mummy doesn't love them anymore if they say no to a request. In some cases, parents have reported that their children tell them, 'I hate you!' No parent wants to hear those dreadful three words, but we must keep this in perspective.

As I stated earlier, children are self-centred. Even in homes where the parenting is balanced, the concept of hearing no can still be difficult for a child because having their needs met is always at the forefront of their minds. This need is so pressing for the child that they will use whatever means necessary to get what they want. If it means upsetting you with those piercing three words then they will do it, not because of how it makes you *feel* but because of what it makes you *do* for them.

N-O-W

The drawbacks with this 'misspelling' are similar to the ones we have just discussed. Children who have not had to learn to wait take that mentality into school where they will not always be first in line, where the teacher has thirty children that he or she has to attend to, where they will have to put up their hand and sit and wait until the teacher can turn to them. The school day alone involves a number of incidences where children have to wait. If the message given from home is that they don't have to wait, they can have it now, it can make regular school activities very challenging for the child – but also challenging for classmates, the teacher and other support staff working with them in the classroom.

Responding to children according to their time frames also reinforces the idea 'my world is about me' when, in fact, parents should be actively trying to teach children to be mindful of others.

I recall being at a friend's house for a meal, where we all sat at the table and ate. My friend's son happened to be the first one to finish eating. He got up from the table and went to get his handheld game console. As he tampered with it, he mumbled about a problem with the battery. As his mum still sat and ate, he said, 'Can you go and get the battery from your room please?'

I know my friend very well and was not at all surprised to see her immediately begin to pull her chair away from the table with the intention of leaving her dinner to get the battery. I also know her well enough to be confident that at times I can interject in an attempt to model a more helpful approach.

So I asked Kevin, 'What is your mummy doing right now?'

'Eating,' he said.

'How about letting mummy finish her food before you ask her to get the battery?'

Tilting his head to the right he said, 'OK.'

It was not a negative exchange for any of the parties involved. In fact, my friend later thanked me and acknowledged that she sometimes goes into autopilot. When children are expected to wait, they learn how to read situations and how to consider when might be an appropriate time to make a request. By modelling this behaviour in the home, children learn what is expected of them.

D-O N-O-T C-R-Y

I must confess that the prolonged sound of a baby crying is something I struggle with as it speaks of an unmet need and defencelessness. Babies are totally dependent on adults to respond to their cry and it is the only language that they have at their disposal to ensure their needs are met. So for me, when I hear them cry I just want to know that the cry has been heard and that someone has responded.

The struggles that parents report to me, however, are not so much related to babies as they are to toddlers and young children. Parents say that when their child cries they see their role as doing whatever it takes to make the crying stop. This can become a very negative cycle for parents and children. What we have to realise is that the idea of having needs met is so important to children that they take note of the things that work. For these reasons parents need to be very careful about showing their discomfort at hearing their child cry. Children will catch on that you will attend to them both quickly and favourably if they cry and cry and cry. You will have met children, I am quite sure, who have realised that crying is a very powerful weapon in their armoury.

It is important to look at each situation and be clear about what is actually occurring. It is quite easy to detect when a child's tears are in fact part of a protest; at these times parents need to hold their ground. Do not try to match the noise that they are making but simply state why you cannot meet the request and remove your attention. For very small children the unmet request and withdrawal of attention may intensify the distress; with these children it is more appropriate to console them and bring a sense of calm, before you explain why the request cannot be met. Also, it can be helpful to acknowledge what your child is feeling by saying, 'I can see that you are upset, but...'

Learn to trust yourself. You know that nothing has occurred that would result in distress so just because the crying is loud and prolonged does not mean it is urgent. Your child will recover from a prolonged tantrum or from prolonged crying. As a parent, it can be hard at first when you are trying to address this particular aspect of parenting; but once the balance is addressed it is well worth it. Perseverance leads to a child having to learn to regulate their own emotions. It also teaches them how to respond more appropriately to disappointment. They learn that being upset is fine, but that there is no need for prolonged crying just because they have been told no.

The last thing I will say on this subject is that it is imperative that we own what is our issue and what is an issue for the child. Most parents know that it is not healthy to parent your child in such a way to avoid situations that lead to tears. Even with this knowledge, many find it difficult to resist this avoidance approach because of how the crying makes them feel. It is important to separate what is happening for your child from what is happening for you. Parenting, as I have described, is shaped by our own childhood experiences: the good, the bad and the indescribable.

Things to think about and do...

♦ How has your experience of being parented shaped how you parent your children?

♦ Children of primary school age need to be taught how to regulate their emotions and recover from setbacks. Practise allowing more and more time to pass before responding to your child's tears.

♦ Give your children specific time frames for when things will happen and then stick to them. For example:

◊ We will go to the park in ten minutes
◊ You can do some drawing in ten minutes
◊ I will come and read with you in fifteen minutes

Chapter Three

What's in the bag?

Starting the day the right way

Consider carefully what you say before you send them on their way

We all have our morning vitals. For some it is a cup of tea, for others a newspaper and yet for others breakfast is the most important meal of the day. There are some things that just help us to start the day the right way.

In this chapter I would like us to consider what the morning vitals are for children. What do *they* need to be best prepared to engage in the school day? Children spend on average twenty-five hours a week, that's approximately one thousand hours per year, in school! I am sure the expectation of all parents is that their children are, amongst other things, actually learning.

Have you considered what you as a parent can do to ensure that when your child arrives at school they are in the best possible place, mentally, to engage with learning?

Think about the general atmosphere in your home in the mornings. Is it a picture of calm, with parents and children leisurely making themselves ready for work and school? Or is it a picture of chaos, where children struggle to find the items they need for the day and adults battle to get children to understand the need to hurry?

It is also worth thinking about not just the start of the day but also the end. Often the problems of the morning are a natural culmination of issues from the night before. So for example, if your son or daughter had a late night there will be a knock-on effect on the morning routine; the energy levels will not be what they ought to. This is a common problem for families where children have TVs and game consoles in their rooms because parents cannot monitor what time these have been turned off and children have gone to sleep.

As a teacher I have experienced first-hand the negative effect that a poor start has on the school day for children of all ages. The issues may vary; children arrive at school ill-prepared because they are hungry, tired, worried or stressed but the outcomes are generally the same – an inability to engage fully in learning.

I recall my friend telling me a story about her nine-year-old son.

'That morning consisted of the usual mad dash to get myself ready for work and Kevin ready for school. I'm generally quite a patient parent, but on that morning Kevin appeared to be moving in slow motion, and after finding him sitting in front of the TV for the third time, the irritation got the better of me. "Kevin, get up and get dressed. You're going to make me miss my train." I didn't shout, but my tone was stern; I could tell from the way Kevin looked at me as he slipped into his trousers.

'There was no apparent coldness between us and we exchanged the usual hug and kiss at the school gate before going our separate ways.

'It wasn't until I collected Kevin from school much later that day that I realised the impact of my words that morning. Our initial greeting was not the usual recount of his day. Instead, the first question he asked me was "Mummy did I make you late for your train this morning?"

'My heart sank. Had that been on his mind all day? As it turns out I was not late for my train at all, but while I carried on with my day at work, my son carried my earlier irritation on his mind. That discovery hurt my heart.'

This picture is no doubt common for most households with school-aged children: the picture of morning mayhem. Trying to organise everyone is a real chore and trying to get the little ones to understand the need to rush is harder still. I am sure that many parents, like my friend, would be troubled to discover that their child was preoccupied during the school day with memories of a negative exchange with mum or dad that morning.

The problem with preoccupation

The look on Erica's face when she walked into my Year Five classroom spoke volumes. Her face looked 'hard' as if it was taking everything in her to keep her feelings in her heart and off her face. She was often late, but today her body language was saying so much more than the usual 'sorry I'm late Miss'. There was clearly something going on. I noticed that she did not make the usual eye contact with her friends and the pep in her step was missing. I gave her a thumbs up as she glanced over at the board and collapsed into her seat. I waited until the end of the lesson, when the other children left for morning break, to check in with Erica.

'You looked tired when you arrived this morning Erica,' I began.

There was no verbal reply, just the trickle of tears flowing down both cheeks. I went over to my desk, lifted two tissues from the box, sat a little closer to her this time and waited.

Erica took the tissues. 'We've been evicted,' she disclosed as she wiped both eyes. 'Last night we stayed in a hostel, but it's quite far away that's why I was late.'

As she told me of the circumstances surrounding the eviction and the uncertainty of where she would be spending the night, I could not help but just stare at her. I was stunned that this ten-year-old girl was arriving at school with so much on her mind. The explanation for her lateness and her makeshift uniform caught me unawares.

Erica was a tough cookie; she possessed an emotional maturity that was way beyond her peers and she fully understood the ramifications of what was going on for her and her mum. The time we spent talking was brief as she was clearly uncomfortable with both her tears and the retelling of the events faced by her and her family. The significant thing for her, I felt, was simply explaining that her lateness was about far more than a lack of organisation as is often the assumption on the part of teachers.

Erica made it through the school day seemingly unhindered by recent events; but how much learning can a child really engage in when they arrive at school so heavily laden, both mentally and emotionally? How much do you really care about the dimensions of an equilateral triangle when you have no idea where you will spend the night?

This is one of a number of stories of children who arrive at school having had the most unimaginable start to the day. Many teachers have now accepted our role is far more than that of teacher, but now has to include: counsellor, surrogate parent, social worker, confidant, the list goes on. As was the case with Erica, the issues facing families are often complex and have not simply been brought about by poor parenting. However, I have also seen children suffering the effects of their parents being unaware of the ramifications of their actions, or indeed inaction.

Show and tell

I remember being a trainee teacher and having to cover a Reception class. As it neared the end of the day, the children would be pulling and tugging at me to make sure that I had not forgotten about Show and Tell. The children were asked to bring items from home, all of which were put into a large sack. At the end of the day it was the teacher's task to pull an item out of the sack and invite the child to whom it belonged to come out to the front and both *show* the class their item and *tell* them two things about it.

The look of anticipation on the faces of the children as I rummaged around in the sack stalling to pull out an item was such a joy to behold. The animation and enthusiasm with which they spoke about their items is something I recall with fondness.

I have also seen the other side of the coin. When children bring 'things' into school from home that they cannot tell anyone about because they barely understand it themselves. They have questions like: Why were mummy and daddy shouting? Why was mummy crying? Why didn't daddy come home? Will grandma be picking me up again? They use their behaviour to *show* and *tell* that they are struggling to carry the load in their bag. How comfortable would you be if the content of your home life began to spill into your child's school?

What's in the bag?

One would expect a child to arrive at school with a bag filled with the necessaries: stationery, PE kit, a lunch box, water and books. More and more, however, children are piling into school with things in their 'bags' that make both the start and the remainder of the day very difficult.

Some are tired because they have not had sufficient sleep. Others are hungry because they skipped breakfast and opted for a packet of crisps and an energy drink en route to school. Still others rock up with minds flooded with concerns about what they have witnessed at home: arguments, family members coming and going with little or no explanation, or the news of a pending divorce or separation. Some children arrive exhausted because of the pressure brought about by extra-curricular activities and excessive homework regimes.

In my previous book I included my poem entitled 'Will You be the One?'. This verse taken from the poem is just a glimpse of what it can be like for children, who struggle to focus at school because of the weight of what is in their bag.

> Will you notice the good as well as the bad?
> You see I come with more than a pen and pad?
> I try to shut them out, but they follow me to class,
> The sound of screams and breaking glass.
> I try to focus… '5+5 makes 10.'
> But then I wonder 'Will mummy and daddy be fighting again?'

Most adults are skilled at keeping a divide between home and work, but children do not have the capacity to separate the issues and leave home issues at the door. It all comes in with them and often teachers meet children at the gate whose 'bags' are weighing them down.

Let us pause here and take a moment to think about your household. Are there some adjustments that need to be made to ensure that your children get off to the best possible start in the mornings? What have you given your child to 'carry' to school? Do they carry a sense of acceptance? Of security? Of being loved unconditionally?

I truly believe that parents are often totally unaware of some of the things that children come to school thinking about…

Not every father is a barber

I feel the need to advocate on behalf of the many children I have met, who wished that their dad would just send them to the barbers rather than attempt to cut their hair. This may seem like a trivial or even comical point, but I write it in all seriousness in the hope that you will hear my heart-felt plea. Not every father is a barber! God bless the many dads who sit their boys down and give them a home-made haircut rather than send them to the barbers. But have you thought about what it is like for them to go to school parading a hairstyle that was clearly not crafted by a professional?

I have seen children in tears, refusing to come into class because they are embarrassed about their hair. Let me quickly add, that the case for girls is not much different. Though it may not relate to a haircut, sometimes parents do not give thought to the types of hairstyles that their children are forced to don. I've seen children crying in class because their braids are too tight, or as a result of having to wear hair extensions that are too elaborate and not age-appropriate.

Consider your child's level of comfort at what they have to walk around school with – whether it relates to hairstyles or attire. Does their uniform fit well? Is it too small or too big? Is there something you have placed on them that could make them feel self-conscious? I implore you to think, am I helping my child to start the day the right way?

Setting them up for success

What have you observed that works well for your children? What could you begin to provide to help set them up for success?

Here are a few suggestions of minor adjustment that can be made to ensure that children get the kind of start that parents hope for.

Prepare the night before. Maybe the constant stress in the morning is because there are just too many things to get done in a short space of time. Are there things that could be prepared the night before?

Part of your child's evening routine could be to pack their school bag ready for the morning. They could even make their packed lunch once they have finished the evening meal. Give some thought as to what could feasibly be done the night before to relieve some of the pressure in the morning.

If we are totally honest some of the stress brought about by the morning mayhem is simply because our expectations are too high as to what can get done in the time that we have before school. If something is not working well, we need to improve it. Start making the change even if it is slow or small.

Enquire about the day ahead. As you sit for breakfast, ask your child about what the day has in store for them. What will they be covering in English today? What is the topic at the moment? Help them to get their minds ready for the day's learning. Choose topics of conversation that are going to stimulate their minds and encourage creativity and reflection. This approach would prove a lot more constructive than children watching TV or playing on game consoles during breakfast as parents then have to tear them away to get out of the door.

Something from the heart before you depart. Try to ensure that your last exchange with your child before you part company is warm and reassuring. If the morning has been manic acknowledge that with your child. Make sure that they are not carrying any feelings brought about by the morning's busyness.

This can be a challenge for parents when there have been ongoing issues at school around behaviour. It can seem more appropriate to send children off with a warning about what will happen if poor behaviour continues. The better approach, however, is to send them off with an expressed expectation that it will be a better day for them. Tell them that you look forward to hearing about it later. No child wants to begin the day with a threat from mum or dad, 'You had better behave today, I don't want to be getting any calls.' This does not set children up for success; it is, in fact, very stress inducing.

There are the very obvious things like a hug and a kiss at the school gate – if your children still regard these things as 'cool' of course! If not, find a way to express affection to your child that is not overly tactile but has significant meaning for both of you. The key message is to release children with no doubt about your love, your acceptance and your expectation that they will do the best they can at school that day. That kind of start sets children up for success.

Things to think about and do...

♦ Over the next few weeks monitor the mood and atmosphere in your house in the mornings. Note your findings and make changes where necessary.

♦ Are there parts of the morning routine that could be moved to the night before to ease some of the pressure?

♦ What would it look like if home life began to 'spill' into school through your child's behaviour?

♦ Make a point of sending your children off to school in a positive frame of mind. What could you say or do to put this into practice?

Chapter **Four**

How many times have I told you?

*The importance of effective
communication*

Children need to be guided by your WAYS and your WORDS

It was Walter Barbee who said, 'If you've told a child a thousand times and he still doesn't understand, then it is not the child who is a slow learner.'

Effective communication is what we say being heard and heeded by the listener. If, as the quote above suggests, the message is not getting through, it is up to us as adults to find an alternative way to communicate it.

In this chapter we will explore the importance of ensuring that communication is clear so that children stand the best chance of hearing what is being said. We will take into account some of the basic principles of effective communication and look at how these principles relate to giving instructions, correction and praise.

What makes communication so tricky for parents is that it can sometimes mean having to adopt approaches that do not come naturally. For example, if by nature you are a passive person, quite softly spoken and reserved, you will discover that at times as a parent you have to take a more assertive approach with your children in order to be heard. Being passive is fine, but it is very important to know when an alternative approach is needed. The same can be said for parents, whose natural approach is a more aggressive, more heavy-handed and emotionally charged response. Aggressive communication can breed fear in children; often with this approach the message is lost in the emotion, making it ineffective.

The best type of communication is delivered assertively. Such communication is clear and consistent, and the delivery is measured and calm. There is cohesion between the message and the manner in which it is delivered.

Why is communication so important?

Many of our attempts at shaping the behaviour of children are done orally: we give instructions, we give correction and we give praise. Though we may not realise it, we are constantly in the business of commenting, feeding back and making suggestions when it comes to the behaviour of children. It is, therefore, of great importance that we spend some time in this book thinking about how this can be done effectively, as well as looking at some of the reasons behind ineffective communication.

First of all, let us look at the three main communication styles that parents use. You may recognise your own style here.

The passive approach

This approach can be summed up in three words: unsure, unclear and inconsistent. Let me be clear, the approach we use in our everyday conversations is not what is being discussed here. I am talking about the communication styles used by parents when giving instruction, correction or praise to children. I make the point because I don't want to appear as though I am saying that being passive is negative; passivity has its place, as do the other approaches we will go on to discuss.

The passive approach to communicating with children often breeds problems because what is said is delivered without any real conviction and is therefore not believable. Children tend not to respond the first time an instruction is given using this style. As with all approaches, the giveaway with this style is the tone – it lacks conviction and urgency. It communicates resignation and uncertainty. Whining and sighing are also associated with this approach; together they communicate a lack of authority and control.

Passivity in parenting

Mike was clearly fixated during the parent workshop where we discussed communication styles; he identified very strongly with the passive approach. He explained the problem he encountered when communicating with his six-year-old son, Kyle.

'Everything has to be repeated over and over. I just find it so hard to get him to do what I need him to do.'

I asked Mike for an example of something he had instructed his son to do without success. He gave me two.

'Getting ready for bed, that's usually where the drama begins. Just getting him up to his room or into the bathroom is an ordeal.' I prompted him to talk me through it and was soon able to see why problems occurred.

'I generally run the bath while he watches his last ten or fifteen minutes of TV and then I call him up.'

I asked how he did that. Mike was puzzled by my question, but I had a feeling that I knew what was coming.

'I say "Kyle, are you ready for your bath now?"'

'Can you see that's actually a question and not an instruction?' I replied.

Many parents are completely unaware of how what they are actually saying to children compares with what they think they are saying. Being clear is the first rule in effective communication and we will focus on this a lot in this chapter.

The result of this passive form of communication for the child is a combination of non–compliance and confusion. Confusion arises from the incongruence associated with this style of communication. So, for example, you say, 'Thomas. You need to go to bed now.' Your tone, however, sounds as though you are making a suggestion rather than giving an instruction. So Thomas does not comply because he doesn't think he has to.

Non-compliance occurs for the same reason. You don't sound sure, so Thomas tests the boundaries by not moving because your tone communicated to him that he has that option. Another classic problem with the passive approach is the tendency to ask questions rather than give instructions.

Questions need to be replaced with a clear instruction to the child. Here are some examples:

Question:	Instruction:
Do you want to go to bed?	It's time to go to bed. Make your way upstairs now, please.
Why are you still up?	I've told you to go to bed. Turn the lights out now, please.
How many times have I told you?	This is the second time I am asking you to... now do it, please.
Why are you playing with your food?	Take your hands out of your plate and eat your food with the fork, please.

Clear statements leave the child in no doubt about what is expected of them. The passive approach is sometimes fuelled by the 'anything for a quiet life' motto. For this reason, parents only enforce some of the rules, some of the time because they do not want to 'rock the boat' and then have to deal with the kickback from more assertive approaches. They don't want to upset anyone or cause confrontation.

The problem with this is that the result is anything but a quiet life! Children become both angry and confused because they do not understand the inconsistency. What was permitted yesterday is forbidden today; what worked yesterday (temper tantrums, whining and crying) does not work today. This leads to legitimate anger on the part of a child. The anger arises because the terms have been changed without warning and what you used to hand over quite readily you now withhold. This approach to communication is both unfair and unhealthy. Children need to be clear about your expectations. They should receive consistent messages from both parents about the dos and don'ts within the home.

The aggressive approach

This style is at the opposite end of the scale to the passive approach. This form of communication is harsh and abrasive and is delivered in a 'do as I say or else' tone. Children comply for a time, not because they understand or consider the point to be of any real importance but because they do not want to face the parent's wrath. The problem with this approach is that it is control through fear. Parents, who use this approach, believe that they have control. I would argue, however, that fear is the underpinning driver for them. Fear, that if they are not aggressive then the control that they have (or believe they have) will be lost.

In short, this approach is not helpful for the parent or the child because it is rigid and forceful. The tone used is harsh and threatening and is usually accompanied by a loud voice. This can cause your child to feel like a victim: a victim of your threats and hostility. It can then lead to children using that very same approach in their outside relationships. Feeling that they do not have a voice within the home, they quickly learn to use aggression to avoid any chance of being a victim of such treatment outside the home. In the context of school, this can be problematic for children because they do not understand why they are being reprimanded for doing the very thing that adults do to them.

In addition, children who are raised in the midst of aggressive forms of communication do not develop the natural curiosity associated with testing boundaries. They are so fearful of the ramifications that they dare not refuse to comply. The problem with this is that the urge to test boundaries does not go away, but instead intensifies because this natural curiosity is not being satisfied. Children often become oppositional and non-compliant in school because they have not had the opportunity elsewhere to test boundaries as part of their normal development.

We would do well in our communication to remember that as adults it is not our privilege to 'lord' our authority over children in a dogmatic and dictatorial way. The first priority is to teach children through our own conduct how to communicate in a way that, above anything else, conveys love and a positive regard. This applies as much to correction as it does to praise. Getting this balance right takes much practice, and more so if your natural approach or indeed your own experiences of being parented have developed in you a proclivity towards aggression. Help is at hand in this chapter!

The assertive approach

The aim is to develop a style that is assertive: firm, but fair. The assertive parent is clear about what is acceptable within the home and they communicate their expectations consistently and in a calm manner. Children feel safe in the hands of assertive parents, whose style is measured and predictable, as it is unlikely that there will be unexpected outbursts.

These parents have understood that assertiveness is not about being authoritarian – as is often the confusion. They see that this approach is by far the most effective way to convey love to children. This approach says: I love you enough to tell you when you are wrong; I love you enough to say no every now and then because I know where overindulgence can lead. It says: I love you, therefore I do not want to leave you in a state of confusion; I must be clear so that you know where you are with me. That is love.

Assertive communication comes from a place of confidence and clarity: it's definite, not doubtful; clear, not clouded; measured, not manic.

Take a moment now to reflect on your own style of communication. What is your natural style? Is if effective with the children? What adjustments do you need to make?

Let's revisit some of the points I mentioned earlier when discussing the passive approach. The passive approach is to ask questions rather than give instructions. The statements given on page 58 in place of the questions are the kind used by assertive parents.

This approach yields long-term results because children actually learn why their behaviour was not acceptable as well as what they need to do to remedy the situation. Parents, who are calm communicators, give their children maximum opportunity to learn.

Giving instructions
Here are some helpful suggestions based on key times when communication can go wrong.

• **Ensure that you have your child's attention** before giving the instruction. So, if the TV is on put it on mute or better still pause it so that you have your child's undivided attention. Bear in mind that if you stand in front of the TV during your child's favourite programme, it is not likely that you will have their full attention.

• **Use an assertive tone** so that your child is clear that it is an instruction and not a suggestion. Consider the words that you use – state, do not suggest. For example 'Take your school bag upstairs please' should be said rather than 'Do you want to take your school bag up now?'

• **Keep the instruction as simple as possible** and use the least number of words. Try not to give multiple instructions at once such as: 'Go upstairs, take off your clothes and put on your pyjamas, brush your teeth, wash your face and get into bed.'

• **Give your child the benefit of the doubt.** If they have not followed your instruction, check that they actually heard what you said rather than assume that they are being defiant.

• **Allow take-up time** after an instruction is given. State what you want your child to do and then move away. Allow time for your child to process what you have said and respond. It can also be helpful to give children a time warning: 'OK, you have five more minutes before lights out.' This communicates that you are fair and reasonable and that you understand it can be hard to withdraw from a fun activity without warning.

• **A logical consequence should follow** if children have not followed an instruction after a number of attempts. Make children aware that if they choose not to do as they are told, they are likewise choosing the consequence that goes with it.

Giving a warning/correction

The key thing here is congruence, as mentioned earlier. It is vitally important that your tone is assertive and communicates a sense of seriousness.

- **Make eye contact and use their name.** This communicates a degree of seriousness. I am sure many of you can remember, as I can, being called by your first or full name by mum or dad and the seriousness that it conveyed.
- **Remain calm** so that what you have to say does not get lost in the way you are saying it.
- **Ask the child to repeat what you have said** to ensure that they have heard and understood. This is important for young children; but does not work well with older children or teenagers.
- **State the consequences of non-compliance.** Ensure that it is clear what will happen if there is non-compliance – consequences should not catch children unawares.

Giving praise

It is important that your manner complements the praise you are giving to the child.

- **Use gestures** to add to what is being said – a thumbs up, a wink or a high five.
- **Use the child's name.** It can really add value to praise.
- **Ensure you have eye contact with the child.**
- **Praise in a way that is appropriate** to the age of your child, but also in a way that does not take away from the positive impact of the message. By this I mean, avoid the temptation to add a comment to the

end of a praise statement. For example: 'Well done for tidying your room; you could have done it a bit quicker though.'
- **Put a smile on your face.** This may seem obvious, but it will go a long way in helping your child appreciate the sincerity of your praise.
- **Ensure that your tone is also bright and cheerful.**
- **Public praise**, particularly for younger children, can also be very effective.

I am sure you have heard it said that it is not what you say, but the way that you say it that counts. As far as communicating with children goes – this is a very true statement. Unfortunately, it is where many of the problems lie in communication – or non-communication – between parents and children. *How* you say what you say is of far more importance than *what* you actually say.

Take responsibility for those times when you have not made yourself clear or you have been inconsistent. Children will respect parents who take ownership by acknowledging mistakes and inconsistencies.

Things to think about and do...

♦ Monitor your communication with your children over the coming weeks. Are your instructions phrased as questions?

♦ Try giving time warnings rather than bringing activities to an abrupt end. Remember to give praise if children finish in the time agreed.

♦ Add 'thank you' onto the end of an instruction. It communicates faith that the instruction will be followed. For example:

◊ Shoes upstairs, thank you
◊ Toys away now, thank you

♦ Admit when you get it wrong and say sorry.

Chapter Five

Didn't I do well?

The place for and the power of praise

A child reaps the benefits of affirming words for a lifetime

Praise is such an important part of parenting. It is the means through which we let children know how well they are doing in relation to our expectations. Praise, when it is applied effectively, acknowledges both achievement and effort, so children at varying stages of development can get a sense of their progress.

Like other concepts outlined in this book, the idea of giving praise can be very difficult for many parents because it is not something they recall receiving as a child. It may well be an approach that has to be learnt and practised; the results, however, are well worth the effort.

Most of us, I'm sure, will acknowledge that receiving praise can be incredibly encouraging and validating. It lets us see that our efforts have been noted. Conversely, when praise is withheld, it may breed resentment because it can give the impression that contributions are taken for granted.

Another reason parents sometimes struggle with praise is because they feel that children should do as they are told regardless of whether or not they are praised for it. They feel that children should not expect praise, but rather they view praise as a bonus – if you get it great, but if you don't, get over it.

In the same way that we let children know when they have done something displeasing, we should let them know when they have done well. Isn't this only fair?

It is vital that children know when they have hit the mark, since pleasing the people who are near and dear to them is of such importance. How else will children know that you are pleased if you do not praise? In fact, good behaviour that is not praised, will eventually stop. This is particularly true with children for whom behaviour is an issue. The reason for this is simple.

Children who have developed habitual patterns of poor behaviour, will have been told constantly by adults that their behaviour is not appropriate and that it needs to stop. In one way or another they will have received attention for their behaviour albeit negative attention. It takes a lot of effort for these children to begin to address these behaviours and make alternative choices. However, when they do not receive praise, their hard work in amending their behaviour goes unnoticed, making the effort not worth their while. As a consequence, they simply revert back to the original behaviours because it brought more attention from adults.

This is a cycle that needs to be broken in many homes: catch them being good rather than pounce on them the minute they make a mistake. Take the time to think about it now. Is there a balance between praise and correction in your house? Are you as quick to notice the good as you are to notice the bad? Don't fall into the trap of thinking that children should immediately remember right from wrong and therefore do not need the affirmation that praise brings. This is a misconception – children know what you teach them; and where rights and wrongs are concerned, they will note what you promote.

If you get animated, annoyed and engage in an argument with your child every time they fail to tidy their room, children will note that. This kind of interaction can be a huge pay-off for some children particularly when it is one of the few occasions that they actually receive attention from you – even if it is in the form of a telling off. Remember, for many children negative attention is better than no attention at all.

It is so important that parents avoid these negative cycles. The giving of praise should be regular, specific and given at the time the positive behaviour is happening. If you notice your children playing together sensibly, say something in that moment, rather than later on. Children need to make the link between your praise and their performance. When they receive praise in the moment they are not having to recall what they did, and the praise maintains its potency.

As a teacher in school, praise was a key part of my behaviour management approach. If a child was off task in my class my immediate response would not be to reprimand that child, but instead to praise a group of children, who were focused and on task. This way my attention was given to the children whose behaviour warranted it. This would very often be sufficient in encouraging the first child to get back on task. Giving praise in this way places attention on the principal thing: the positive behaviour adults want to see more of.

Let's break it down and be really clear about what it is I am saying about praise. A definition is a good place to begin.

What is praise?

Praise is defined as 'the expression of approval or admiration for someone or something'.

Think about this definition for a moment. How does it make you feel when someone approves of you? It's a great feeling, right? To know that someone likes you or what you are doing, to know that you have found favour in someone's eyes, to know that in that moment you have someone's acceptance and support. How important have these interactions and experiences been for you as an adult? Even writing this I'm reminded of friends and colleagues in my own life who have affirmed me, encouraged me and commended the work that I do. If I'm being really honest, I'm not sure that I would have made it this far without them – they have been vital to my development, both personally and professionally.

Why in the world would anyone want to withhold praise from children? The only sense they have as to how well they are doing is the feedback we give them. Praise is vital, I say it again, *vital* to a child's development and sense of self. To know that mummy and daddy approve of them is every child's heart's desire. If they are unsure of this it can make relationships difficult as there is then a void, which they will seek to fill.

When should we praise?

In a word – often! It is said that for every word of criticism, children need three words of praise to reset the balance. In short, children should be praised more than they are criticised. Again, if you think about your own life as an adult, it can be very draining to be constantly criticised by your line manager or fellow team members. It is like taking a verbal battering day in and day out. Such an existence is not healthy for even the toughest adult much less a vulnerable child.

If you see your child do something that is praise worthy, don't hold back – praise them. In fact, cast your eye over everything that your child is doing and actively look for things to celebrate and acknowledge. Use praise to encourage children to continue with difficult tasks like tidying up. Don't wait until everything is cleared away – praise them as they go along. They will feel motivated to continue because their efforts are being noticed.

It can also be a huge encouragement to a child when they are praised in public. It makes them feel extra special that you have seen fit to praise them in front of other significant adults.

Get into the habit of praising everyday things are well as huge achievements. Here are some examples:

- Coming in from school and carrying out the routine – uniform off, packed lunch put away, etc
- Making their bed in the morning
- Getting out of the bath when asked
- Sharing with a sibling

How to praise

It is key that your praise sounds genuine. So, it is important to include gestures in your praise to ensure the child gets the message that you are pleased. In the case of praise – actions *do* speak louder than words.

Praise with a smile on your face and with an upbeat tone. It is also very helpful to establish meaningful gestures with your child that communicate approval as mentioned in the last chapter. That could be a thumbs up, a high five or a wink, to name a few. Also, it is so validating to use the child's name and to make eye contact when praising.

Praise and behaviour

Praise becomes even more important to children for whom behaviour is an issue. It can be so easy to become stuck in a rut of constantly nagging your child about their behaviour in a desperate attempt to convince them to change. Unfortunately, that is not the kind of approach that brings about a change in behaviour. In fact, children change their behaviour in response to the changes adults make in their handling of them. It starts with you.

Where there is a problem with a child's behaviour, sit down and identify where the difficulty lies. Once parents are clear about the issues, behaviours then need to be tackled one or two at a time. The suggested approach is not to consider how the child can be punished when the negative behaviours occur, but instead make a point of praising and rewarding the times when the child makes a more positive choice about how they will behave.

So, for example, if the problem is around the use of negative language or rudeness towards adults, you would look for times when your child responds politely. When such behaviour is observed, it should be praised and/or rewarded. The child then begins to note the benefits of making a more positive choice about their behaviour: mum and dad are pleased, the atmosphere at home is more positive and they receive recognition for how hard they are trying to behave better. This response to behaviour difficulties is far more constructive and helpful than simply continuing the negative cycle.

Rewards

The use of rewards can be a contentious topic, but I do believe there is a place for rewards in the management of behaviour within the home. We cannot justify the use of consequences without also giving consideration to what happens when children get it right. I think it is worth stating that I am not in favour of children being rewarded for things that parents have a right to expect, like compliance, speaking politely and observance of agreed rules and routines. For me this is where the use of praise should suffice.

I believe rewards should be given where children have found behaving appropriately very difficult; for them the idea of getting it right is a much bigger deal than for the average child. In such cases, the reward (agreed with the child) should be something that they can work their way towards. So, for example, where a child has fallen into the habit of not following bedtime instructions, a chart could note when the child responded to the request to go to bed the first time it was made. Each time the child responds appropriately, put a star on the chart. Once this positive behaviour has been sustained over an agreed length of time, the reward should be issued. The reasonable amount of time to wait for a reward is largely dependent upon the child's age. Younger children of primary age will need to see the reward sooner than older children, who have a greater capacity to wait.

The best approach is to agree the parameters with the child and especially what they would like as a reward. What is a reward to an adult may not be a reward to a child. A word of caution here – it is best to develop a bank of rewards from which a child can choose, rather than leaving the choice wide open.

I remember carrying out a survey in school as part of my role as behaviour lead. I wanted to find out from the children what kind of rewards they would like to earn for good behaviour. The survey was carried out with all the children from the Reception class (aged four and five) right up to the eleven year olds in Year Six. The results were insightful. The older children's requests were pretty standard: extra playtime and extended time on computers to name a few. The feedback from the Reception children was as you would expect from four and five year olds; but I was struck by two in particular. One child said they would like a smile for good behaviour, while another requested a hug! My point is this: children need and want to be validated and praised when they do well. Find a way to praise that is appropriate for your child's age and is personal and meaningful to them.

Rewards do not have to be elaborate but could be any combination of the following:

- Extra time on game consoles
- Time at the park with a friend
- The purchase of a small item that is in line with the child's hobby/interests
- A quantity of money – e.g. one pound – that can then be accumulated to buy something bigger later
- Time playing outside

Parents can also choose at any time to add to these rewards as a way of saying well done to a child, who they can see has been making a huge effort.

Remember that rewards should not only be used with children for whom behaviour is an issue as more compliant children could begin to feel as though it is more worthwhile being challenging. You may well have a child for whom compliance is commonplace; rewards should also be used here as a way of acknowledging a child's consistent effort or tendency to make positive choices.

Try to ensure that all the children in your home get equal attention, praise and rewards. Don't fall into the trap of going overboard with a difficult child in an attempt to win them. You may well win them, but in the process lose others. Parenting needs to be balanced; children for whom good behaviour comes easy as well as those who find it difficult should frequently receive the praise and recognition they need and deserve.

Remember, for children behaviour is only worth repeating if there is a perceived pay-off. Children can find it very difficult if they are being asked to stop doing something that for them is actually meeting a need.

So when they partner with you in trying to amend poor behaviours, praise their efforts readily.

Children who are brought up in the same households with the same parents can still be very different in their behaviours. Many parents become bewildered when one child behaves so differently to a sibling. What parents have to be careful of is that the compliant child doesn't start to think that they have to begin to misbehave in order to receive rewards. These children should be enjoying all the niceties that come with being respectful, compliant and trustworthy. Such benefits should form a part of their day-to-day existence. They may not need a chart where their efforts and achievements are tracked in the same way, but at the very least their efforts should be recognised and rewarded. In fact, it is helpful for children in both these situations to observe the rewards of positive behaviour as well as the consequences of negative behaviour.

Praise is powerful, praise is validating, praise is vital to every child's development.

Things to think about and do...

♦ This week focus on how you praise effort as well as achievement.

♦ How can you ensure that your children are praised (three times) more than they are criticised?

♦ What will your response be when your child turns negative behaviour around? Remember to notice and praise.

♦ What praise or reward can you offer?

Chapter Six

Can we please agree?

The need for partnership in parenting

Where the partnership between parents is weak, the potential for manipulation is high

Consistency is far more than saying the same thing over and over. It is the same thing coming from different mouths. Being in agreement about the 'how' of parenting is more important than many parents and carers realise as it's often not until children begin to display the poor behaviours consistent with a weak partnership that a problem is acknowledged.

Abigail, a parent who attended one of my courses, had been really motivated by a session looking at why challenging behaviour occurs. In particular, she was struck by the concept that if you permit something within the home, by default you permit it outside the home too. Abigail stood with her husband Steve, as she explained the difficulties they had been having with their twelve-year-old daughter, Justine.

'We are a little too relaxed about her swearing, I must admit. Justine just finds it really hard to express her anger or frustration without swearing at us. We do pull her up on occasions, but we have let things slip.'

'Actually if we're honest, Tracey,' Steve quickly added, 'it's not just when she's angry. Sometimes I hear her on the phone talking to her friends and she's quite happy to drop the odd swear word in here and there, not because she's angry but because she can get away with it.'

Abigail continued, 'The problem now is that we are getting complaints from Justine's school about her foul language. I know it sounds silly but it didn't occur to me that she would talk like that at school.'

The conversation continued and revealed further inconsistencies on the part of Abigail and Steve. Not only had they not considered that it was only a matter of time before Justine would take her use of foul language outside the home, they also appeared surprised that their daughter was using the very same swear words that they, as her parents, used to one another.

I explained that the problem was the mixed messages Justine was receiving from them, her parents. Abigail and Steve left the session in complete agreement that things needed to change. I was encouraged by their expressed commitment to work together to improve things.

The following week I scanned the room looking for Abigail and Steve as I was keen to get an update. Abigail had come on her own this time.

It transpired that although Abigail believed they were both in agreement, the events of the week revealed a nonchalance on Steve's part that was not consistent with his earlier admission that things needed to change. Abigail looked dejected as she told me about one of the conversations she had overheard between Justine and her dad.

'They were in the kitchen preparing dinner and Justine was talking to her dad about school. I don't think they realised that I was in the passageway sorting through the mail. She described a friend of hers as a f*****g idiot because she had caused them both to get a detention. I waited for Steve to challenge her, but it didn't happen.'

Abigail's voice raised slightly as she continued, 'I've really stuck my neck out this past week: pulling Justine up in precisely the way that Steve and I had agreed. As a result, I've really felt the strain in my relationship with Justine, but I remember what you said about it getting harder before it gets better. That's the thing, Tracey, I just don't think Steve is prepared to put in the hard work – he doesn't want to be the bad guy.'

Acknowledgement and application are not the same. Acknowledging the need for change is a vital first step to addressing inconsistencies in parenting, but that must be quickly followed by the application of effort to remedy the situation. Many fall down at this hurdle.

Let's further consider just how vital it is for parents, whether living together or apart, to have an agreed way of raising their children.

I am a firm believer in the power of partnerships, both professionally and personally. Ecclesiastes, one of the wisdom books in the Bible, puts it like this:

Two are better than one,
because they have a good return for their labour:
If either of them falls down, one can help the other up.
But pity anyone who falls and has no one to help them up.
(Holy Bible, New International Version, Biblica, Inc. 1973, Ecclesiastes Chapter 4, verses 9-10)

Where there are two parents within the home, the only real way to yield the kind of results that many desire is to be in agreement. What makes the winners of a three-legged race effective is their ability to create a rhythm and flow. They start off slowly, but once they establish the rhythm of their partner and anticipate the timing of the movement, they are off and create their chance of winning.

Partnership cannot be established where there is little or no knowledge of how people tick. There needs to be some prior knowledge of what the other person stands for when it comes to parenting.

Where the priority for both parents is a strong partnership the results can be far reaching; conversely, where the partnership between parents is weak children will, in most cases, take full advantage of this and limit the chances of success.

I laughed as my friend told me how her three-year-old daughter had managed to get one over on her dad. 'My daughter came into the living room licking an ice lolly. It was as if she was licking it in slow motion to in some way depict the sheer delight she felt about having an ice lolly against my wishes. I had earlier told her that she could not have one because it was too close to dinner time. So she did the classic thing and went to ask her dad. It was a hot day, so he saw no issue in saying yes. When I asked him why he had allowed our daughter to have the lolly he apologised and said that he didn't realise that she had already asked me.

'For me the issue here was two-fold – he should have checked with me that our daughter hadn't already asked me because this had become a recent habit. The other, bigger issue is that I would expect him to know that I would not allow her to have an ice lolly at that time of the evening. He should have known that I would not do that. We talked about it again later and laughed because we realised that our little angel was in fact no angel and that she was very busy looking for the weak link in the chain or even the tiniest crack that she can slide through to get her hands on an ice lolly or anything else that her heart desired.'

The starting point for partnership

Effective partnership begins with a discussion and an agreement about what is going to be acceptable within the home. This dialogue is very important because it is at this stage that both parents have the opportunity to put their proposed view and approach forward, so that by the time it is communicated to the children there is agreement. The following points may form part of this discussion:

- Agreed bedtime
- Curfew
- Rules and routines
- Chores
- Mealtimes (chores, routines, at the table or in front of the TV?)
- Acceptable language/lifestyle

Without these initial agreements there is no real basis for partnership because you have not established how things are going to work on a daily basis.

Agree what is acceptable for your home, for your child. I emphasise this because so often parents agree to things that they do not actually believe in simply because friends or relatives run their own home in that way. There is certainly a place for learning from others where parenting is concerned, particularly from those who have wisdom and experience to share. That does not negate the need to be clear and certain as to your own standard and your own way. They are your children and they live in your home. Do not put yourself in a position where you are trying to enforce something that you do not believe in. It creates unnecessary work and tension.

Partnerships can be difficult to establish in cases where parents do not reside in the same home, particularly where the relationship is strained. The best thing that parents can do for their children, even in cases of divorce and separation, is to protect them as best as they can from the emotional entanglement and prioritise their best interests. This can be achieved by following through with agreed behaviour expectations.

Good cop, bad cop

In many homes where there are two parents one is perceived as the bad cop, while the other one enjoys the glory associated with being the good cop. The bad cop enforces the boundaries: their yes is yes and their no is no. The bad cop is not easily flattered by hugs and kisses and the classic baby voice that children often use to try and get their way.

The good cop is the one who will eventually say, 'Oh go on then, one biscuit won't hurt.' They desire to be a problem solver, so they will want to be the one to make things alright. Sometimes this leads to inconsistency and frustration on the part of the bad cop, who is working hard to keep to the agreed rules. The good cop is more concerned with how they are perceived by the children and they will compromise the partnership if it leads to popularity.

Let's look at another example from Alan and Michelle, the parents of Zane.

'I was like the dragon lady in the home,' Michelle said. 'I worked evenings, so Alan was responsible for settling Zane for bed. I would come home from work at eleven o'clock and find Zane up in his room playing on his game console and Alan in the living room playing on his. This was very infuriating as it felt like I was coming home from a shift then having to work another shift trying to get Zane to settle for bed. It's even more frustrating hearing Zane say, "Yes, but dad said I could stay up." I wanted to throttle the both of them!

'It got to the point where I would delay coming home from work because I knew what I would be facing. After a while it just became too much hard work and I gave up the fight. Zane's bedtime routine became non-existent and it wasn't long before his tiredness began to affect him at school.

'For us, the time at the Summer School was life changing because by then both Alan and I realised that we had raised a monster and that if we stood any chance of fixing things we had to be united. I remember the session called Consistency – Keep On, Keep Together that Tracey led. I remember we were asked to discuss the areas where we felt we needed more support from our partners and I just broke. The frustration and disappointment had been pent up for so long, the tears just came flooding. I think Alan was shocked, not just at my reaction but at what we were all hearing about the impact of partnership.

'We made some decisions that day that I am proud to say even to this day we have stuck to. Zane has a bedtime routine that we both stick to. There were temper tantrums at first and I'll be honest, there were times when Alan and I were very close to the edge, but we stuck it out. My household has never been as peaceful as it is now.'

A word of caution for the good cop…Your glory will be very short lived because though they often resist boundaries, children actually feel much safer among people who do not move and shift. You will have the top spot for a season, but children more often cleave to the one with whom there is certainty and safety because it's the place where they feel most secure.

Consistency clarified

Consistency simply means to keep on doing the same thing. Once the agreements have been made and approaches decided upon, it's about doing and saying what you have agreed to: all the time, every time. So, if swearing is wrong today, it is wrong tomorrow.

Ownership is really important here: ownership of your part, your role and your contribution. Avoid giving children the impression that you want to sanction their request but that you have to side with your partner. So, phrases like 'If it was up to me, I would say yes' should be avoided because these do not promote partnership but instead erode it. Such statements give the impression that there is no real buy-in to the idea of partnership, but suggest instead that the priority is to undermine.

There may well be occasions where as a parent you have a different view to that of your partner. You may feel that what is being administered to your child is unfair. It is not advisable to express that opposing view in front of the child; rather, wait for a time when the matter can be discussed in private to preserve the partnership.

It can be difficult to persist with systems and routines when things do not appear to be working as expected. Where working together and establishing consistency is a new approach it will take time for both parent and child to become accustomed to this new way of being. It's important to persist, particularly where you feel strongly about what you have decided. Conversely, as children grow older and develop maturity and responsibility it is good to review the rules and routines within the home to ensure that they are still suited to the age of the children and their stage of development.

Things to think about and do...

♦ It's much easier for children to follow through and be consistent if they see it modelled by you.

♦ How much of what you expect *from* children do you demonstrate *to* children?

♦ If you have a tendency to undermine your partner – take some time to consider what your underlying reasons might be.

♦ How can partnership be strengthened? Consider:

◊ A review to establish what is working well and what needs to be changed
◊ A discussion with the children to ascertain their view
◊ Making a fresh start if things have slipped

Chapter **Seven**

How far is too far?

Setting limits, enforcing boundaries

Life without limits is lethal

A number of things around us have limits: how fast you can drive, the amount you can withdraw from a cash machine in a day, the number of minutes you can talk on your mobile phone for free. Limits are set, among other reasons, to keep people safe. Where children are concerned a life without limits is lethal.

My mum had a saying when we were growing up: 'Too much of one thing is good for nothing.' That is actually very true: too much sugar, too much salt, too much freedom, too many restrictions – they can have disastrous consequences. I think you see the point I am trying to make about parenting – it's about balance: love and limits, rights and wrongs, dos and don'ts. As important as it is to praise children and reward their efforts, it is equally important for parents to set limits to what is expected and accepted within the home. When these limits are clearly stated and consistently enforced children feel safe. This does not mean they will not kick against these boundaries, but ultimately they learn that the boundary is immovable.

Mr and Mrs Folake

The Folake household was a busy one with four children all under the age of ten years. Mrs Folake explained why, with this number of young children, she could not afford to be casual about boundaries.

'In our house it has to be clear otherwise we invite chaos,' Mrs Folake began. 'The children know that they can play in the garden, their bedrooms or the dining room but not in the living room. We do not compromise on that. We are also crystal clear about hitting and swearing – it is not allowed here. They have to find other ways to sort out problems between one another, for example by using words to make their views known.'

I was impressed with how clear Mrs Folake was about the way she ran her house, but I also appreciated her honesty about the fact her children still tried to push the boundaries.

'Yes, on occasions I have caught my boys play-fighting in the lounge, but we have got to a stage where I have to say very little, the expectations are clear and often a reminder is enough. They do try to push it from time to time and if they could get away with it, I'm sure that they would do it more. Their dad and I are a good team; we work together and the children know that.'

Consistency and behaviour

When it comes to the management of behaviour, consistency is non-negotiable. Behaviour within the home cannot be managed effectively without a clear set of boundaries agreed and enforced by united parents. I lose count of the number of parents I have met who have tried to go about it in other ways and have failed miserably.

Positive behaviours need to be both taught and caught. Children need to be told but more importantly they need to be shown. When you combine consistency with the modelling of positive behaviour you are onto a winner. I was amazed at how many of the parents on *Mr Drew's School for Boys* swore in front of their children but then told their child off for swearing! You do not have to be a parenting or behaviour expert to know that this simply makes no sense. Your child will pick up positive behaviours far more quickly if they are modelled by you.

Consistency can be one of the hardest things to establish, but one of the easiest things to lose; it takes real work to keep it going. This is why the discussions at the outset are so important. They establish the rationale for rules and routines and allow the non-negotiables to be agreed from the start. Parents are more likely to hold fast to something that they genuinely believe in, because when you understand why something is important you do not let it go easily.

Be careful to ensure that consistency is maintained especially during times of stress and pressure. If, for whatever reason, boundaries become loose – acknowledge with the child/children that things have not been as you would have wanted and let them know that things will be returning to normal.

Without such a discussion, parents can be perceived as being very unfair in the eyes of children, who have been led to believe that what they were doing was acceptable because it was not being challenged. This can lead to both resentment and anger.

Consequences do not work well when children are taken by surprise – they should know in advance what will result from poor behaviour choices. The ultimate aim is for consequences to work as a deterrent.

Without wanting to sound contradictory, I think it is also important to mention the need for flexibility even in the midst of a consistent approach. Children have different temperaments and this needs to be taken into account when it comes to dealing with behaviour. For example, some children do not respond well to public reprimand because for them the idea that they have disappointed a parent is catastrophic. In this instance, it would be more supportive to speak to the child in private rather than discuss the matter in front of siblings. Other children may require an immediate firm reminder about expectations because that is what works for them.

The point you want children to remember is that consequences follow poor choices. However, if your child is so distraught because of the approach you have taken this key lesson will be missed. Being flexible is not about changing an expectation of behaviour but rather about flexing the route that you take to arrive at the enforcement of an expectation.

Even when children have made mistakes and their behaviour disappoints us, they are still worthy of respect; even the application of a consequence should be done with due regard for the child's feelings.

Rule setting

The best way to set limits within the home is to have an agreed set of rules, which everyone is informed about. These should be displayed in a communal part of the house, such as on the fridge, where they can be easily accessed and referred to. The best approach to rule setting is collaboration rather than dictation. However, it is important for the adults to agree first of all what their expectations are before sitting down as a family. The discussion should be twofold: What rules do we want to have? Why are these rules important? Even in this collaborative approach, parents should not be afraid to state the non-negotiable expectations. There will be some things that must be enforced regardless of how children feel about it.

A set of rules might include:

- Speak positively to and about one another
- Clean up after yourselves
- Food is eaten in the kitchen/dining room only
- TV up to eight o'clock on school night
- Treat people how you want to be treated

Notice that this sample set of rules is positively phrased – they state what should happen rather than what should not. You want children to focus on the positives: what *is* permitted, what they *can/should* do and what their parents *are* looking for in their behaviour.

Generally, you will need a set of rules that deal with how people will speak and behave towards one another. Rules should also cover any restrictions around times and locations – for example, where and when meals are eaten. There will, of course, be many other rules within the home, such as curfew, time allocated for the use of mobile phones, laptops and other technology items and things around the house the children should not touch. But the core set of rules should be brief, clear and memorable. For that reason, there should be no more than five or six agreed rules for the house. Children cannot be held accountable for what they don't know and they can only know what they can remember.

Rules that cover the agreed conduct within the house should apply to both adults and children. There is no point having a rule that says we speak politely to and about one another and then as parents you shout and swear at one another. That communicates hypocrisy; double standards do not go down well with children, who are far more likely to comply with rules if they see them being upheld by the adults within the home.

Once the boundaries have been set it is important for the adults within the home to work together to embed them. If one party begins to slip up by allowing the children to eat in front of the TV for example, this slip up should be acknowledged with the children and the boundary 'reset' so to speak. Mistakes must be owned by adults and quickly remedied because the longer they are allowed to go on the more confusing it will be for the child when you begin to enforce the boundary again.

The agreed set of rules should be referred to regularly with children being praised for compliance and consequences quickly following non-compliance. If there are no consequences for breaking the rules, then the rules are pointless. It should be seen as a natural occurrence and understood that by virtue of choosing to break a rule, children choose the consequence that follows. This is a vital lesson in cause and consequence that, if they do not learn as children, they will certainly learn as adults, by which time the consequences may be far more costly.

One of Aesop's fables tells the story of the young thief and his mother. A young man had been caught in an act of theft and was condemned to be executed. Before meeting his death, he made one final request to see his mother. When she entered, the young man called his mother near as if to whisper something in her ear. When she drew near the son lunged at her almost biting off her ear!

As astonished onlookers gasped in disgust, the young man said, 'I did that to punish you because when I was young I started stealing little things here and there and instead of correcting me you laughed and said it would not be noticed. I blame you that I am here now.' The same moral is reflected in the following verse from Proverbs in the Bible:

> Train a child in the way he should go and when he
> is old he will not turn from it.
> (*Holy Bible*, op. cit., Proverbs Chapter 22, verse 6)

Children need to learn these vital life lessons at a young age: that choices have both positive and negative consequences, that sometimes they have to wait, that they can recover from hearing the word no and that they must take responsibility. This area of parenting is worth maximum investment because children prepared for life in this way grow up to be adults, who can function in the wider world and make a positive contribution to society.

This process, however, should be approached with certainty not severity. Children do not need to be yelled at or lectured when they break a rule because when the yelling stops no lessons are learnt besides the fact that rule breaking leads to anger. Instead, what the child needs is to face the logical consequences of their actions. When rules are clear and consistently enforced you should simply be able to ask them what happens when they don't turn the TV off at eight o'clock. They should be able to reply that they lose fifteen minutes TV the next night. It's as simple as that. Application of rules needs to be clear not severe.

Routines

We cannot talk about rules without talking about routines because it is the routines that enable the rules to be held in place. In simple terms, routines are a sequence of actions that are regularly followed to provide predictability and order.

Routines should complement the set of rules within your home. So, with reference to the sample set of rules on page 92, appropriate routines could be:

- Make bed before breakfast – enforces the rule that we clean up after ourselves
- Children help to set the table – enforces the rule that there is a place and time to eat
- Bath and book before bed – enforces the rule that TV goes off at eight o'clock

A child's need for structure and predictability cannot be overstated. By providing children with boundaries and routines you are creating the kind of environment within which they can really thrive. It is the knowledge of an agreed order of things together with your consistent enforcement of the rules that creates the sense of safety for the child.

Think for a minute about how it makes you feel when your bus to work is diverted or you have to take an alternative route because of train problems. This kind of disruption can be both annoying and anxiety inducing because you are thrown from your usual routine. We grin and bear these disruptions, but they can make even adults feel ill at ease.

It was my friend, Tina's birthday so a group of us headed to a local restaurant to begin the celebrations. Janet told us to go ahead while she stopped at the cashpoint. We were seated and began chatting and scanning our menus. About fifteen minutes had passed before I said, 'Where is Janet?' We concluded she must have had to walk further down to find a cashpoint that was working and we continued our conversation. It was close to twenty-five minutes before she returned, clearly confounded.

'They've changed the cashpoint!' she blurted out as she plonked herself into a seat. 'I put my card and PIN in, but then my card came out of the machine straight away, so I thought there was a problem. Then my name came up on the screen and I thought "Woah, what is this?" It threw me! They have changed it all and it's taken me this long to work out what on earth I was doing!' We laughed at the utter confusion that had been caused by a change in a routine procedure. Some changes cannot be avoided and will happen without warning. Adults do bounce back, but children need the consistency of routine and a warning, if possible, when things are going to change.

One of the key times of day where parents struggle to enforce boundaries is bedtime. A look at this in more detail should prove helpful.

Bedtime

For many parents this is a testing time where children seem to come up with the most elaborate excuses as to why they do not want to go to sleep or are not tired. It is important to note here that some very legitimate anxieties can arise for children at bedtime: separation from parents, fear of nightmares and a concern as to what might happen to parents while children are sleeping. Allow children to have nightlights if there is an anxiety about the dark; stuffed toys can also provide comforting companionship.

There could of course be a much simpler explanation for resistance at bedtime; children may just not be tired owing to a nap taken earlier in the day or maybe their bedtime is too early. It is important to take all of these factors into account when setting bedtime routines or dealing with resistance.

The following routines can be helpful at bedtime:

Winding down: Overstimulation at bedtime is counter-productive as it excites children when they need to be calming down. Consider carefully the activities that children engage in before bed and whether they bring calm or excitement. It is said that both the activity and bright lights from most game consoles overstimulate the brain – they are not an ideal part of bedtime routines.

In February 2015, an article in *The Daily Telegraph*

carried the headline, 'Banish smartphones and computers from the bedroom to get a good sleep, say scientists'. The article went on to state:

> The bluish light screens emit can prevent sleep because it mimics daylight, convincing the brain that it is still daytime.
>
> (*The Daily Telegraph*, 2 February 2015)

Ideal routines could include: a bath, reading to or with children, playing a quiet word game and listening to calming music. The predictable order of these routines can also be soothing for children, so it is worth keeping the routine the same for the most part.

Give warnings: About ten to fifteen minutes before bedtime approaches, give your child a warning that it will soon be time to go to bed. Issue a second warning at around the five-minute mark and then make the last minute or few seconds playful. For example, you could say: 'Who can beat the clock?' 'Can you get upstairs and into bed before I count to twenty?' These games take the sting out of the fact that it is bedtime and can help to minimise the resistance or sadness that can set in.

Hold the boundaries

If children persist in saying that they are not tired at bedtime but instead say they are thirsty, hungry or scared be clear about how much of these tactics you are prepared to give attention to. You may decide that they can have a little drink or snack but be very clear that the expectation is still for them to go to bed. It can help to set up an agreement with your child that you will come in and check on them in ten minutes, but warn them that if they get out of bed before that time then you will not come.

Taking this idea a step further, part of the bedtime routine could be two 'check ins'. You agree with your child that you will look in on them at ten-minute intervals to check that they are OK. Do not establish this routine if children are perfectly happy to settle themselves at bedtime; it can, however, help reduce anxiety for children who find bedtimes particularly difficult. It is vitally important that where these 'check ins' are agreed that parents keep their word.

It may be necessary to set up a system of rewards if bedtime problems persist. For example, you could set up a chart where children are given a tick or a sticker if they go to bed the first time they are asked, or if they settle after their two check ins, or lastly if they do not get out of bed at all for the night.

Changes to routine

If routines are going to change it is helpful to let children know in advance. So for example, if mum or dad is going to be working late and not joining the family for dinner children should be told this in advance rather than having to work it out for themselves based on the empty seat at the dinner table. A minor change for an adult could be a major change for a child. So as far as is possible the more children can be forewarned about things the safer they feel.

When routines slip because of an event like visiting family or being away on holiday, acknowledge that things have been a little different for a while, but now they will be going back to normal.

One parent I worked with called Mr Taylor, reported, 'For us it's the school holidays that we need to be careful about. It's so easy to let your whole routine fall apart when schools are out. We make a point of getting back into the routine a few days before school recommences and this involves a conversation with the kids. We ask them what they have enjoyed most about the holiday and my wife and I don't have to tell the kids about routines, they tell us! We ask them what happens now that the holidays are over and the kids talk us through all the routines that are back in place because it's the end of the holidays. This approach seems to work really well.'

Giving instructions

Coupled with enforcing rules and boundaries giving instructions is an important practice for us to think about in this chapter. Children need constant reminders about rules and routines which will involve having to repeat instructions. I would like to offer some guidelines to ensure your instructions are heard and heeded. Consider the following:

- **Do you have your child's full attention?** Teach your children to *show* that they are listening by insisting on eye contact.
- **Does the tone you are using match what you are asking?** So, for example, if your tone is playful when you say, 'Off to bed now boys,' you may not get any take up.
- **Ensure that you give an instruction rather than ask a question.** 'Go to your room now please,' rather than 'Would you like to go to your room?'.
- **Keep instructions simple and use as few words as possible**. It is best to say, 'Tidy the toys away now please Rachel.' Avoid saying, 'Tidy the toys away please Rachel. How many times do I have to ask you and look at the state of your clothes, why are they so dirty?' The

principal thing is the directive to tidy the toys away, but two further points were made that could cause the initial message to be lost. This type of approach can lead to an overload that leaves the child confused as to what it is you are asking them to do.

• **Allow take-up time once an instruction is given.** Give your child time to process the instruction and carry it out – this should only be a matter of seconds. Try not to turn a situation into a stand-off where you give an instruction and then you stand over your child until it is carried out. This can be deemed as confrontational from the child's point of view and depending on your child's temperament, they may deliberately resist purely because you are standing there. In a way you have invited confrontation and they are simply accepting the invitation. It can also be very powerful to add the words 'thank you' to the end of an instruction because it conveys high expectations of the child's behaviour.

It can be difficult for parents to feel comfortable with the idea of boundaries particularly where there are memories of over-authoritarian parents or conversely memories of a very loose, casual approach to parenting that they believe didn't cause any harm. In any event, children need parents who are not afraid to set limits and boundaries, which will help them grow into adults accustomed to order and structure in their lives.

Things to think about and do...

♦ Do you need to take some time out to establish a set of rules for your home? Which of your house rules has become obsolete?

♦ What will you apply from the suggestions in this chapter to improve the bedtime routine?

♦ What boundaries have you set with your children? How consistently do you enforce them?

♦ How many times do you give warnings and follow through?

Chapter **Eight**

How will you know if you don't go?

*Understanding how schools work and the
need to stay connected*

Our experiences of school shape our approach to parenting more than we think

School can be a daunting place for the parent of the 'naughty' child. For them school is a place full of people who hold a negative view of their parenting. It's the place where their child is nothing but an inconvenience and where teachers believe strongly that they, as the parents, are to blame. In all my years of teaching and working with children and their families, this has never been made clearer to me than when I worked with the parents on the programme *Mr Drew's School for Boys*.

The very thing that would normally have the potential to divide a group of parents was actually the very thing that held the group so tightly together – the fact that they were all parents of children with behaviour difficulties. It was the parents' unanimous view that it made such a change for them to be in a room with other parents whom they could relate to. Many of them shared stories of how judged they felt by teachers and other parents at their child's school. Here is Ruth's story.

Ruth Carr – mother of Max

'It got to the point where I couldn't bear going to the school. I know it was wrong but I would let my daughter drop Max off and pick him up. It's a combination of what people actually say and what you assume people think of you. I was always conscious that my Max was the naughtiest child in the village and yes, for a short while I thought it was quite cute; but it wasn't long before I felt alienated and it began to affect my relationship with the school. I fell out with the head teacher because he didn't approve of Max's blonde Mohican; but I didn't see the problem with it. When you feel persecuted and judged it just makes you dig your heels in more because you believe that everyone is against you. I felt as though it was me and Max against the world.

It wasn't until Stephen and Tracey led a workshop about the importance of the home/school relationship that I realised how unhelpful my behaviour was. As a head teacher, Stephen Drew helped me to understand how difficult it can be to work with parents, who are so resistant and think that the school is just trying to get at them and their child. I got so much from that session and declared live on TV that I would seek to improve my relationship with my son's school. I have since met with his head teacher and cleared the air. I also no longer allow my daughter to take Max to school; I drop him off and pick him up myself.'

In a January 2013 article featured on the online resource, Teacher Toolkit, Stephen Drew wrote:

> ... please accept that when we teachers tell you that your son or daughter did this or that, or indeed didn't do this or that, we are not 'out to get him' or 'picking on her'.

In the aptly titled article, 'Dear Parent, what I'd like to say is...' Drew concluded by saying:

> ... this is what we are here for sometimes; to hold your child to account for their actions and to work with you to help your child learn from what they have done so that they can grow and develop as a young person and be better for the experience. So please don't say 'my child would never say that' or 'it's clearly a clash of personalities'. Both of these statements are profoundly unhelpful and completely undermine what we are trying to do to help your child.

Stephen Drew has articulated what is the heart's cry of most if not all teachers: a deep desire to work in partnership with parents, who understand and support the school's intentions towards their children.

In this chapter I want to explore the importance of a home/school partnership while acknowledging how hugely difficult it can be for some parents to cross that threshold into their child's school. This difficulty, I have discovered, can be brought about by ongoing issues with a child's behaviour or because of a parent's own childhood experience of school. You will know from your own experience that memories of school linger for many years. I have led a number of workshops for both teachers and parents where I have seen tears shed as people recalled their own memories of school.

There is often a direct correlation between a parent's experience of school and the quality of partnership between that parent and their child's school. In some cases, recalling their own parents being very hands-off with their schooling can lead to an overzealous and overprotective approach to their own parenting. The bottom line is that whether we realise it or not we have been impacted by our own experiences of school – be it positively or negatively. These experiences can colour your view of teachers and affect how you relate to them.

Here is another story from a parent featured in *Mr Drew's School for Boys*.

Sarah Fielder – mother of Spencer

'My mum and dad never came to my school. School was like the no-go zone. I don't quite know what the thinking was behind it, but there seemed to be this unspoken law that said, "We'll deal with home, but when it comes to school – you're on your own." Thinking about it now I do believe it has impacted on how I parent Spencer, including my relationship with the school. They would probably describe me as a pushy parent – one who is always sticking her nose in and asking questions.

'I never miss a meeting at Spencer's school and I try to encourage his dad to do the same. I have had to fight for Spencer because I have often felt that his teachers did not understand his ADHD. I felt like I was in a fight with the school, particularly his primary school where the latter years for Spencer were really difficult.

'Stephen and Tracey's session that looked at our experiences of school was both emotional and insightful for me. I didn't realise how impacted I was by my own parent's lack of engagement.'

Impact of your schooldays

Both Sarah and Ruth's stories are very common and a key lesson I learnt from working with them is that it is not helpful to judge people: to presume that they are just being pushy or protective. As part of our role as teachers, we need to seek to build bridges not create obstacles to partnership.

The workshop referred to by both Ruth and Sarah involved Stephen and I presenting some key thoughts. The parents then had to reflect on their experiences at school and consider how true a series of statements were for them, for example:

- There was at least one adult that I trusted at school
- I was supported by my parent/s with my schoolwork
- I had a number of friends during my schooldays
- Most of my teachers were positive about me
- My feelings about my time at school influence how I speak to my own son about school

Why is partnership important?

Where there is partnership there is a joined-up approach when it comes to schooling and parenting. When a child knows that teachers and parents are in communication they are less likely to try and play one off against the other. It makes the job of teachers in schools hugely difficult when parents hold a negative view of them and share that view with the child or air it within the child's hearing. I know a number of teachers who have had to contend with children coming into school saying, 'My mum said I don't have to listen to you!' This may surprise some, but it is a very real and unfortunately common experience for teachers.

Partnership makes the job of both teaching and parenting much easier as one can provide vital support for the other. Children have to adhere to rules and routines at school; where this is echoed at home it makes it much easier for children to comply with expectations in both settings. Support from parents around punctuality, homework and arriving at school equipped for the day is so vital to help children learn to be organised and manage their workload at school.

The homework debate

We realised that there were a number of parents at the summer school who had issues with homework. One dad asked why, if his son did work at school all day, did he need homework? Stephen and I decided to run a session entitled Why Homework? which we hoped would give a platform to both sides of the debate. I had no idea the session would get so heated.

The rationale for homework was put forward by one of the teachers and included an explanation that it allowed children to practise key skills at home.

A very strong case was also offered as to how unhelpful it can be to the child when parents refuse to insist that they do homework. It was clearly stated that parents who do this were actively working against teachers in schools and causing their children to incur sanctions such as detention.

Some of the parents went as far as to say that they felt teachers were, in fact, deliberately trying to make life difficult for parents by issuing homework. Some also believed it was a reflection in some way on the teachers' inability to do their job, when children had to continue work at home.

It must be said that though the views were varied and strong there were in most cases legitimate arguments both for and against homework. The common theme was a lack of awareness of the impact that a negative attitude can have on the partnership with school. Parents seemed taken aback when teachers explained how parents being uncooperative about homework might be perceived.

As I sat and listened I was stunned by how strongly parents felt about this issue and how far some of their views were from reality. What later emerged, however, from one of the most vocal parents during this particular debate was an underlying feeling of inadequacy and fear.

Alan's story

'I felt like a dunce at school and because I found reading and writing difficult I was pretty much discarded by my teachers. I was placed in a class with other "special" kids and never really made to feel as though I could achieve or get better at the things I found hard. When you have that kind of experience in school you just shut off. I played around in school and I didn't have any real interest in learning because no one had any interest in me. As soon as I was able to leave – I did.

'So now, with Zane, I do avoid going to his school because I feel like I don't know anything. All the memories come back and so I just create an argument about everything to avoid having to go. I know that Zane has picked up that negative attitude from me – he doesn't care about his homework because I don't care about his homework and I know that's not right.'

This chapter title, How will you know if you don't go? was inspired by my conversations and experience with Alan. He is a typical example of a parent who can be grossly misunderstood because of how he communicates and behaves. Given the chance and a safe space to share his story you soon discover that lying just behind the confrontational persona is fear, shame and regret.

Stay connected and informed

Even as I write this most schools are on summer break and in a matter of weeks many parents will experience the unspeakable relief of the schools resuming for the Autumn Term. But what do parents really know about what goes on there? You hang around waiting for the bell to ring, you plant a peck on their cheeks and then you're off; but what happens for the next five hours – do you know? The sad reality is that too many parents have disconnected themselves from school. Part of my objective with this book is to encourage such parents to re-engage.

Education is an ever-evolving sector and it is important to keep up to date. I am not talking about the need for parents to read all the latest articles and publications. For example, you might make an effort to attend parents evening, special assemblies, school plays, school trips and other meetings that will help you to stay connected and informed. It can and does make such a difference to your child when they see you taking an interest in school. It gives such scope to wider conversations about school around the dinner table or on the journey home.

Whatever your experience of school, I urge you to seek to be informed about your child's school in whatever way you can. Try to make some minor changes that enable you to be more connected. Here are some ideas:

• Read the school newsletter when it comes home.
• Make a point of taking your child into the school grounds so that you can get to know names and faces. Ask your children who is who.
• Ask your child about their day with reference to specific subjects and don't be afraid to ask for clarity if they mention something that you are unsure about.
• In most cases children like explaining things to their parents about school.

I know for many parents this is a somewhat idyllic picture as work demands do not permit you to attend meetings as often as you would like. My encouragement to you is to prioritise the meetings that are going to have the most impact on your child. I know, for example, the heartache that is felt by some children when they sit at the front in a school assembly and scan the crowd in a desperate search for the face of mum or dad only to discover that it is not there. Maybe this is the only meeting that you can attend, but take it from me – it would mean the world to your child, especially for those whose behaviour is challenging. You being there because you want to be there not because you have been called in speaks volumes to a child.

Things to think about and do...

♦ Are the key school dates in your diary/calendar: assemblies, trips, performances, etc? If not, why not put them in now?

♦ Make a point of talking to your children over breakfast about what the school day has in store.

♦ If you have concerns about your child's school or teacher, make a point of not discussing these in front of children but agree another time and place when children are not around.

♦ Remember that it is in the best interest of teachers, parents and children that there is strong partnership between home and school.

Chapter Nine

Why can't he sit still?

The joys of parenting boys

Boys want to be trusted more and accused less

A good friend of mine is expecting her first child. Early in her pregnancy we went out for lunch. 'I feel much more equipped to parent a girl,' she began. 'But if it's a boy – I will have to come to you!' My love for boys is no secret – I find them delightful and fascinating. Their boundless energy is a joy to behold and their cheeky attempts at humour are sometimes clumsy, but so cute. By their nature they are risk takers, competitive and active. I have caught myself chuckling on a number of occasions as I've watched parents walking their young son and daughter to school; one in each hand. Usually the girl is walking by her mum's side while the boy is skipping and jumping with mum trying desperately to cling on to his hand. Sound familiar?

In recent times the term 'boys will be boys' has come to carry something of a negative connotation. There appears to be a perpetuating view that boys being boys equals boys behaving badly. In the context of school they are often the ones in trouble and virtually all of my coaching work in schools is with female teachers, who find groups of boys problematic. Primary schools, in particular, are facing a huge problem attracting males to the profession. According to the government publication, *Statistical First Release: School Workforce in England November 2014*:

- 74% of teachers in schools are female
- 91% of teaching assistants are female
- 79% of auxiliary or other support staff are female
    (*Statistical First Release: School Workforce
        in England November 2014*, SFR 21/2015
    Department for Education, July 2015, p.7)

This means that 78% of the workforce in state-funded schools in England is female.

I mention this because it is important for parents to be aware of the context within which their sons are educated; the change in dynamic brought about by a female-heavy workforce cannot be denied.

So what is it about boys? I would like to offer what is an honest, albeit sad, conclusion: boys are among the most misunderstood groups in society.

In her book, *Boys Should be Boys*, Dr Meg Meeker wrote:

The world has grown sad for our boys.
(*Boys Should be Boys: 7 Secrets to
Raising Healthy Sons,* Dr Meg Meeker,
Regnery Publishing, 2008, p.10).

I wholeheartedly agree. Let's look at some statistics from the 2007 publication, *Gender and Education*:
• 70% of children with identified Special Educational Needs (SEN) are boys
• Boys account for 80% of permanent exclusions and three quarters of fixed-term exclusions
• Boys are nine times as likely as girls to be identified with Autistic Spectrum Disorder
• Boys are four times as likely as girls to be identified as having a behavioural, emotional and social difficulty (BESD)
• Boys from Black Caribbean, White/Black Caribbean and any Other Black background are proportionately more likely to be identified with BESD
(*Gender and Education: the evidence of pupils in England*, Department for Education and Skills, 2007)

Boys in school

A head teacher asked me to come into her school to deliver a training session for staff. She said, 'Please could you talk to my staff about how to get the best out of boys. I just feel that when it comes to boys there is more to them than meets the eye, but I'm not sure that my staff know how to capitalise on the unique qualities of boys and use these to maximise their engagement in learning.'

This has also been my experience as a teacher in schools. In addition, many teachers seem to view the natural characteristics of boys as challenging.

I once heard teacher and gender-based education expert, Abigail Norfleet James say,

> Boys will be boys, but the way boys naturally express themselves is a problem for many teachers... Boys get the message that typical boy behaviour: loud, competitive and physical is bad and that they should be more like girls: quieter, cooperative and gentle.
>
> (Young, Drifting and Black Conference, June 2010)

Many teachers are unaware of their subconscious tendency to suppress the very nature of boys. Author Lucinda Neall in her book, *Bringing the Best out in Boys* shares the responses to boys that she observed in a primary school classroom.

> ... When it came to the other boys, the 'boyish' boys... there seemed to be a problem. She was impatient and irritable, nagging and reactive. She had no empathy with their boisterous energy, it was unwelcomed in the classroom and she tried to suppress it.
>
> (*Bringing the Best out in Boys*, Lucinda Neall, Hawthorn Press, 2002, p.xviii)

I wonder if the case is the same within homes? Is your home a place where your son can freely express his need to engage physically with his environment: to run, leap and test his physical capabilities and strength through action and adventure? These are all natural needs for boys, but as is the case in school, they are often suppressed and seldom understood. So, why can't boys simply sit still?

The biology of boys

Boys are more active than girls. They spend more time in motion, while girls spend time in communication.

> Our learning style didn't fit the way we were taught. Our high energy was a minus, not a plus. Our need for movement, for less talk and more 'doing'... did not generally fit the schools we went to.
>
> (*The Minds of Boys: Saving our Sons from Falling Behind in School and Life*, Michael Gurian & Kathy Stevens, Jossey-Bass, 2007, p.7)

Typically, boys also observe in a more focused way whereas girls have a wider peripheral vision. It explains why a boy can walk into the kitchen to get a drink and not see that there is rubbish on the floor. Or why he may put his dirty dish in the sink and not notice that the washing up has already been done and that he therefore needs to wash his own dish.

When it comes to brain function, girls can easily think and feel at the same time, whereas boys tend to do one or the other – making it more difficult for them to express what they are feeling.

Another key physiological difference between boys and girls is the balance of hormones affecting their bodies. Testosterone levels fluctuate through the childhood of a boy and reach their peak at around fourteen. When these levels begin to rise at around age eleven, boys can become, albeit temporarily, quite clumsy and disorganised. According to Meg Meeker:

> A thirteen year old experiencing fluctuating testosterone levels, finds dribbling a soccer ball a bit more difficult – he feels clumsy and awkward. His legs are longer, his gait feels uneven. He needs to correct this, to ease his frustration, and he needs encouragement from his parents to do so until puberty has served him better.
>
> (Meeker, op. cit., p.96)

Testosterone also produces the following characteristics in boys: energetic and boisterous behaviour, self-confidence and a deeper desire to take risks and test boundaries, both physical and hierarchical. These characteristics need to be recognised and managed.

Boys and behaviour

The need to understand boys is particularly important when it comes to behaviour because this is an area where the expectations placed on boys are often unrealistic and in conflict with their nature. When we take into account the natural make-up of boys – we must make the necessary adjustments to our own expectations and indeed our capacity to contend with noise and the general busyness of boys.

Let's look at some of the typical behaviours of boys and consider how we can respond in a way that appropriately and positively accommodates their needs. I am conscious that I have thus far made, and will continue to make, generalisations about the differences between girls and boys with references as to 'typical' behaviours. There are, of course, both girls and boys whose behaviour falls outside of these conventions, but I simply want to address the behaviours that in my experience cause boys to encounter problems.

Boys have a tendency to be reckless and they are often in the middle of an action before they have considered the consequences. They can also be impulsive and loud.

What boys need are plenty of opportunities and outlets for these expressions and clear guidelines on how far is too far.

Boundaries for boys cannot be woolly – either something is forbidden or it is permitted. Anything less than this degree of clarity will cause frustration and confusion for a boy. Also, in situations where boys have overstepped the mark or broken a rule – they need a clear logical consequence, rather than a pep talk. Girls typically become tearful at the realisation that their parents disapprove of their behaviour and for them a pep talk following rule breaking can be sufficient to get the message home and create a deterrent. Boys on the other hand because of their tendency to take risks and their impulsivity need consequences to be a little more concrete – more black and white. The pep talk, if used, must be followed by a consequence in order for it to be effective.

Giving boys instructions

As mentioned earlier, boys tend to focus on one thing at a time. Therefore, on occasion they will genuinely not have heard your instruction if it was given while they were engrossed in an activity. So, in order to ensure that boys both hear and heed – consider the following approaches:

• **Ensure you have their attention** before you issue the instruction. Call their name and wait until they have stopped what they are doing before you start speaking. If they insist that they are listening even though they are not making eye contact, simply say 'You may be listening with your ears but I need you to listen with your eyes.' This is a good principle for boys to learn about effective listening in any context – show people you are listening by making eye contact.

• **Try to use the least number of words possible** as boys will become agitated if something is unnecessarily long and drawn out; it can quickly sound like nagging. This is not a suggestion to dumb things down but rather to just say what needs to be said, for example: 'Bed in fifteen minutes.' 'Shoes on the rack.' 'Coat on.'

• **Be instructional rather than suggestive** to help boys to 'catch' what it is you are saying – if something sounds like a suggestion, boys will treat it as such. For example: 'Do you want to come and have dinner now?' is suggestive, while 'Jamie, turn off the TV and come to the table for dinner', is instructional. Congruence is so important for boys because when your tone matches your talk there is less for boys to have to work out on their own. Boys need us to speak to them with our whole bodies – with words and gestures, as this makes the process of understanding much easier.

• **Ask younger (primary-aged) boys to repeat back** what you have said after you have stated an instruction.

• **Allow take-up time** for them to follow an instruction. Conversely, if the instruction needs to be followed right away be sure to say so.

Praise and approval

Boys like to test their abilities and push themselves to their physical and psychological limits so it is important for them to have a clear sense as to how they are progressing. Praise and approval need to be frequent, specific and genuine.

Meg Meeker says:

> Sons try to please their parents when they know that they can please their parents. Without balancing love and discipline, boys are lost.
>
> (Meeker, op. cit., p.23)

When boys get angry

Expressions of anger from boys need to be appropriately managed. Boys can at times scare themselves with how quickly they become angry. The language that is used in response to their displays of anger is therefore important. Boys need to understand that anger in itself is not wrong, but that some of the behaviours that accompany angry outbursts are not permitted. The following phrases are important because they make the expectations clear:

- You can be angry, but please do not damage things
- You can be angry, but please do not be rude
- You can be angry, but please do not swear

The overarching message that boys need to hear is that anger is permissible but within an agreed set of boundaries.

Boys want to be trusted

Often the biology of boys can get them into trouble because of their tendency to do first and think later. As a result their behaviour can sometimes be perceived as intentionally negative or defiant. The response to boys, therefore, needs to be less accusatory and more enquiry. If, for example, your son is sitting down staring into space rather than doing his homework, don't make the assumption that he is aware of what he is doing. State the facts rather than accuse: 'You have been sitting for twenty minutes and you still haven't started', rather than 'Why are you wasting time? Stop being lazy and get on with the work.' Say what you can see, rather than give your opinion about what is going on. Facts speak for themselves and form a good basis for an honest conversation.

Boys want to be trusted more and accused less. Consider what the behaviour may be telling you about what a boy needs. When boys grow up in an environment of support and understanding they find it much easier to ask for help and admit that something is hard. If they anticipate a hostile response they will try to work it out for themselves leading to frustration and anger.

Boys need to feel valued

When the needs of boys are catered for it makes them feel valued and understood and puts them in a much better place to reciprocate that sense of value and respect. When adults create opportunities for boys to satisfy their need for excitement and competition, they are less likely to feel the need to create those for themselves. That is why outdoor play is so important for boys and is far more beneficial than sitting in front of the TV or playing on a game console for hours. They need to expend energy in constructive ways – otherwise they try to expend energy in the house by turning the living room into an assault course!

One of the main things that boys complain about is things not being fair. They have an acute sense of justice and will struggle in situations where there are inconsistencies by adults which are not addressed and acknowledged. Try to be fair in your dealings with boys.

- Allow them to have a fair hearing in instances where things have gone wrong.
- Administer consequences fairly to all the children in the house.
- Do what you said you were going to do. If you say Johnny can have ten more minutes outside playing football, be sure to follow through.
- In cases where things cannot be the same for all the children in the house because of a child's need – explain so that boys understand why.

Some boys view inconsistencies as weakness; parents who do not fairly and consistently apply rules will struggle to get respect from boys.

Things to think about and do...

♦ How tolerant are you to the nature of boys? Do you need to make some adjustments to your expectations?

♦ When you consider the amount of time your son spends on gadgets compared to how much time he spends outdoors – is it balanced?

♦ Make a point of doing something with your son that he enjoys – this will show him that he is valued.

♦ Remember that anger + anger = more anger! Be a role model to your son when it comes to anger management.

Chapter Ten

What will your mum say?

A parent's perspective

One of the hardest things for parents is when the behaviour at home and in school is so different

I have on numerous occasions been the bearer of bad news. I have been that teacher, who at the end of the school day is scanning the playground looking for mum or dad with whom I need to 'have a little chat'. Maybe you have felt that sinking feeling as the teacher makes her way across the playground in your direction? Maybe you have been one of those parents praying with every step that the teacher is not approaching you; that this time it is someone else's child who has had a bad day?

I have never experienced that feeling personally. This issue is nonetheless very significant for me because, while I may not have had to parent a problematic child, I have been the problematic child whose parent was frequently called into school to hear accounts of my challenging and defiant behaviour.

My schooldays were chequered with exclusions. Even at primary age I had begun to gain a reputation as someone who 'needed firm and consistent handling'.

I have countless copies of school reports which include varying degrees of detail about behaviour incidents that date back to my latter primary school years. The incidents were frequent and carried a similar theme of defiance and insolence towards adults. I am spoilt for choice as to what to share in this book, but here are a few excerpts from some of my reports:

Tracey needs extremely firm and consistent handling. (1982)
Tracey is cheeky and insolent. (1986)
Tracey's attitude and difficulties with self-discipline continue to prevent her reaching her full potential. (1987)
Tracey displays aggressive behaviour to staff and does not accept responsibility or correction. (1988)

In the midst of this dismal picture stood my mum: a woman who had consistently taught me and my four siblings the difference between right and wrong. She taught us that adults were to be treated with respect and school was the place we went to learn. It was as simple as that. So, how does a parent feel when they have done their bit? When they have applied their best effort to raise respectful and well-behaved children and yet they still find themselves in the head teacher's office?

A mother's story

Read on to discover what my very own mother had to endure as a result of my behaviour at school. She tells how it made her feel as a parent and how her experiences have shaped her own perspectives as a professional working with challenging children.

Little Miss Jekyll and Miss Hyde

It was almost as if Tracey had two personalities: one she displayed at home and one she saved for school. What I saw was a well-mannered child, who was respectful and helpful at home. She was not a child who displayed any form of difficult behaviour at home and I always received positive reports from relatives whose houses she frequented. She was personable, humorous and responsible. Though a little forthright, she knew how to stay within appropriate social boundaries. You can imagine my horror when I began to receive letters and reports from school describing my daughter as: insolent, aggressive, defiant and eventually, as someone whose behaviour put her at serious risk of permanent exclusion. These teachers were describing a child that I did not know; behaviours that I had never witnessed. This was difficult to deal with, difficult to hear and often difficult to believe.

Some of the incidents involved disagreements between Tracey and other children and these were a little easier to process because issues with friends are commonplace and a natural part of school life. I remember one particular occasion when Tracey came home with a letter from her primary head teacher. The letter stated that she had been involved in a fight and as a result was excluded from school for three days. I was mortified. Tracey was in her last year of primary school at the time and I was in disbelief that her behaviour had resulted in an exclusion from school.

I had to attend the back to school meeting and I remember the shame as the details of the incident were explained: each word falling on me like hailstones. There were yet further storms to face – they increased in both intensity and frequency. I had no idea that this exclusion, as painful as it was, would be the first of many.

More trouble ahead

Tracey's transition into secondary school was smooth. She was friendly, popular and confident and I was therefore not surprised by how well and how quickly she settled in. I did notice that both of her school reports from the first year mentioned Tracey's need to apply herself more. One teacher said, 'Tracey's progress has suffered due to erratic concentration and effort.' My response at the time was nothing more than a pep talk and a request for Tracey to try harder. Unbeknown to me Tracey had by this time already developed a reputation as a challenging pupil. As she later progressed into her second year (now known as Year Eight) the meetings, letters and exclusions became a regular part of our lives.

Following a brief period of being on report, Tracey incurred an exclusion. This was the first of many incidents where Tracey would be excluded for displays of defiance and a lack of regard for authority. Tracey had apparently been in a textiles lesson and refused to stop taunting a pupil who kept falling asleep. Tracey was asked repeatedly to stop but continued. She was subsequently told to leave the lesson, but refused, causing the head teacher to have to come and personally remove her. I was dumbfounded at this display of defiance; the news of the three-day exclusion did not go down well at all. I spoke to Tracey very strongly and told her that this behaviour was not to become a pattern. My words appeared to have fallen on deaf ears, as within a few weeks there was yet another exclusion.

This time it was a phone call informing me that Tracey had refused to leave the netball court at lunchtime. She had been told that she was not permitted to take part in the netball training that was being offered to pupils during the lunch break. The deputy head teacher went on to tell me that rather than leave the court as she had been instructed, Tracey proceeded to disrupt the entire training session. She refused to go to the head teacher's office, but instead stayed and mocked the teacher. Tracey again required a senior member of staff to remove her from the scene. Another three-day exclusion ensued.

By this time I was very concerned about Tracey's behaviour as it seemed that what I thought was a blip at the end of primary school was, in fact, the beginning of behaviour patterns that were a complete mystery to me. Her behaviour towards the PE teacher was inexcusable and by this time I was confronted with the realisation that my daughter had a serious problem with adult authority in school. Though I was disappointed and dismayed, I did believe that the sanctions imposed would be sufficient to help Tracey curb her behaviour. How wrong I was.

Where was I going wrong?

It was as if the floodgates had been opened: the phone calls, letters and exclusions just kept on coming. There was a further exclusion for an incident with another pupil on the bus to school. The meetings became more difficult to attend as I was bombarded with questions I simply couldn't answer. Do you know why Tracey is behaving like this? Are there things going on at home? The truth was, at the time, I did not fully understand the reason for Tracey's behaviour and I had no idea where that kind of defiance came from.

I questioned myself on many occasions and I felt frowned upon by some of the teachers as if there was something deficient about my parenting. If the truth be told – there were times when I felt that Tracey was being singled out and that incidents were exaggerated. Tracey was quite honest when it came to giving her account about her involvement in things, but there were occasions when she ardently denied being involved and I believed her. It was as if some teachers were trying to crush her confidence and punish her for being popular. There was a fight at the local bus station on one particular morning and though Tracey was not present she was still called into the office. There was a lot of talk about 'Tracey's influence' and her 'leadership abilities' and I do believe that the school at times made an example of her and treated her harshly.

I have a vivid memory of the day the head teacher told us that Tracey was not permitted to go on a four-day school journey with the rest of her form class. I did not agree with that decision at all. I felt it was unfair and unrelated to any behaviour incident. There was another occasion when Tracey and a group of friends from school had rehearsed a dance that they were to perform in a show at the school. Once again, Tracey was told that she could not take part, despite having a main role in the dance. I felt that these decisions were made more to hurt Tracey; this was very painful for me as a parent.

For the most part however, I was supportive of the school and felt that they were genuinely concerned about how much time Tracey was wasting. Teachers were often astonished that Tracey could clown around for the majority of a lesson and then apply herself for the last fifteen minutes and still complete work to a reasonable standard. I grew weary of hearing, 'If Tracey spent more time working and less time chatting she would make a lot more progress.' It was disconcerting and I felt Tracey was wasting her potential.

Close to the edge

The secondary school that Tracey attended had a 'three strikes and out' policy. This meant that once your child incurred three fixed-term exclusions they would be permanently excluded. Following Tracey's third exclusion there were extensive talks at the school as to what would happen. The threat of permanent exclusion hung over our heads like a rain cloud and I was worried sick at the prospect. As a parent you feel powerless when sitting around a table with a number of professionals, many of whom had experienced my daughter's defiance first-hand.

At one particular meeting the head teacher had compiled accounts of all the incidents that Tracey had been involved in that term; it was not very pleasant reading at all. The thrust of the argument was that Tracey had not managed to curb the behaviour habits she had formed at the end of her primary education. There was nothing I could say – the paperwork said it all.

The head teacher eventually agreed to allow Tracey back into school on a modified timetable. She was to report to her head of year twice a day and get her report card signed. One of Tracey's teachers, her form tutor I believe, advocated very strongly for Tracey and offered her support in helping her to stay focused and manage her behaviour.

The teachers were genuinely concerned about how her behaviour was affecting her academic progress and spoke passionately about their desire to help Tracey turn things around. The relief was immense. I know that even Tracey realised that we were very fortunate to have avoided permanent exclusion.

I believe this experience was a bit of a wake-up call for Tracey and I certainly became more vigilant and inquisitive as a parent about how things were going at school. Tracey also appeared deeply touched by how strong an advocate her form tutor was on her behalf. I noticed that a very positive relationship began to develop between them. Tracey started to have more good days and utilised the support offered by her form tutor. She became better able to express herself and began to use her sporting and music talents more readily at school. Things did not change overnight – there were regretfully two more exclusions, but Tracey again managed to avoid permanent exclusion.

Though Tracey did eventually leave school with a good number of GCSEs – it was at times excruciating having to listen to account after account of your child's disrespectful behaviour – behaviour that you yourself do not condone. Those meetings were hard going and they have caused me to sympathise with parents of children who have difficulties at school. For eighteen years I worked in a school for challenging children and I believe that my experiences with Tracey helped me to be more hopeful and patient with children who struggle with behaviour. I would often hold the thought that if my child could use adult support to turn her behaviour around, then the children I worked with could do so too. When parents would throw their hands up in despair and say, 'I don't know what to do with him!' I could easily relate to their anguish, but at the same time offer hope.

Parents of difficult children have a tough time – with all eyes on you, you feel judged, embarrassed, inadequate and at a loss as to how to fix things. It's worse when your child is perfectly behaved at home and then plays up at school – you have to take the teacher's word, you have to picture your child doing something that is alien to your experience of their behaviour.

It is nice to have come out the other end. Tracey and I can laugh about certain things now, but at times it was as if she was oblivious as to the trouble she had caused me. Her main concern, when I was going to be attending a meeting at her school, was that my outfit was coordinated! What can I say? She's my daughter and I love her.

Things to think about and do...

♦ Query the feedback that you receive from your child's school – you should be hearing when things go right as well as when things go wrong.

♦ If you know you have to attend a difficult meeting at your child's school take notes and consider taking someone along for support.

♦ In the midst of difficult conversations emotions can run high – how can you ensure emotions do not cloud/distract from the main issue?

Conclusion

Change will come

I have ended the book with my own and my mother's story because it clearly illustrates that change can happen. When I think back to my schooldays, I laugh at the irony that I now coach and train teachers and parents to help them manage the difficult behaviour of children. I'm sure many of the adults who had to contend with me back then had no idea what I would become. Inspiring hope is a big part of my work with parents/carers and teachers. Having an expectation that things can change is vital for parents facing challenges raising children.

I hope that the pages of this book have inspired you to find the kind of courage needed to make a change. One thing my work with children has taught me is that children change their behaviour as a direct result of adults changing their behaviour towards them. They change because we change. When parents choose to focus their attention on positive behaviour, children in turn begin to show more of that positive behaviour because they can see that it is pleasing and that their efforts to make adjustments are recognised and rewarded. Are you stuck in a rut? Is your house filled with the sound of nagging parents and angry children? Consider how you can change your responses to your child's behaviour to model what you wish to see.

Not only is it important to address difficulties that may be emerging, it is also necessary to put the subject of behaviour at the forefront so that there is some intentional thinking about it when things are calm. I believe parents and carers, like teachers, need to be talking about behaviour daily, whether directly or indirectly. At every turn, children need to know where they stand; it is the job of adults to teach them. Our role as adults should be proactive rather than reactive: not simply correcting negative behaviour (reactive), but more importantly teaching positive behaviour (proactive).

A number of children arrive at school with attitudes and behaviours that make life difficult for them and for those who have to work alongside them. In some cases, these children have not been taught the rudimentary rules of engagement: listen when someone is talking, wait your turn, say please and thank you, or take responsibility for your actions. In the busyness of running a home these things can be deemed as unimportant and therefore become forgotten or overlooked.

In the same way children have to be taught how to eat with a knife and fork or how to tie their shoelaces – they need to be taught how to behave. One of the most significant aspects of parenting is to do it with love and compassion and not with anger – an aspect I hope this book has highlighted.

When children cross the threshold into school they enter a place where the boundaries are clear and expectations for behaviour are high. It's a place where adults heavily rely on parents to instill similar values at home. It's a place where huge numbers of people, children and adults, have to learn to coexist, to socialise and communicate. It's a place where teaching and learning are the principal aims.

I have written this book to invite you into the world of schools to help you better understand how important you are to the work that we do with your children. Let us join our efforts in ensuring that your children get off to the best possible start – that they understand their need to make positive behaviour choices, solve problems, recover from setbacks and manage their own emotions. Development of these qualities sets children up to function well in their relationships, contribute to the world of work and live happy and fulfilled lives.

About the Author

Tracey Campbell is the Director and Lead Trainer of Together Transforming Behaviour Ltd (formerly known as Be the One Transforming Behaviour Ltd). She works with teachers, parents and children providing consultancy, training and coaching in behaviour management.

Tracey also designed and delivers the Behaviour Basics Programme for Parents: a series of six workshops exploring the reasons behind behaviour and the remedy for when it becomes hard to manage. Her programme featured in the 2014 Channel 4 documentary *Mr Drew's School for Boys*, where parents committed to a four-week summer school designed to help them regain control of the behaviour of their sons. As the resident behaviour consultant on the show, Tracey led parents through her Behaviour Basics Programme with astonishing results. She later featured on ITV's *This Morning* and BBC Radio 5 Live discussing the impact of her work with parents at the summer school.

The success and popularity of her programme has led Tracey to provide training to The Channel 5 Parenting Group as well as parents employed within the Viacom Media Networks.

Tracey runs the Behaviour Basics Programme in a range of organisations and schools; she also works with parents within the home.

With over twenty years' experience working with children and young people, and as a former teacher, Tracey is passionate about behaviour management; she knows first-hand the powerful effects of establishing a strong partnership between school and home.

Her first book *Will You be the One? Touching the hearts of teachers, changing the lives of children with challenging behaviour* was published in 2012.

To make enquiries about the Behaviour Basics Programme for Parents please get in touch with Tracey at www.togethertransformingbehaviour.com